LIVINGSTONE

A BEGINNER'S GUIDE

PETER TURNER

Hodder & Stoughton

A MEMBER OF THE HODDER HEADLINE GROUP

Orders: please contact Bookpoint Ltd, 130 Milton Park, Abingdon, Oxon OX14 4SB. Telephone: (44) 01235 827720, Fax: (44) 01235 400454. Lines are open from 9.00–6.00, Monday to Saturday, with a 24-hour message answering service. Email address: orders@bookpoint.co.uk

British Library Cataloguing in Publication Data
A catalogue record for this title is available from The British Library

ISBN 0 340 84541 4

First published 2002
Impression number   10 9 8 7 6 5 4 3 2 1
Year   2007 2006 2005 2004 2003 2002

Cover photo by Bettman/Corbis
Typeset by Transet Limited, Coventry, England.
Printed in Great Britain for Hodder & Stoughton Educational, a division of Hodder Headline Plc, 338 Euston Road, London NW1 3BH by Cox & Wyman, Reading, Berks.

CONTENTS

MAPS

ACKNOWLEDGEMENTS

The author wishes to express his sincere thanks for the help given by Judith Johnson, Helen Nicholson, and Betty Turner; also to Karen Carruthers and Betty Brogan of the Livingstone Institute in Blantyre, to Canon Fergus King of the USPG, to Andrew Young and Mike Brocks of the CMS and to Sylvia Coombes of the Council for World Mission.

The author alone is responsible for any views expressed in the text.

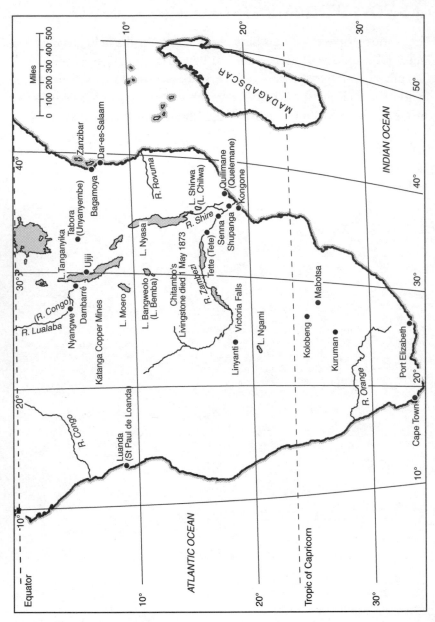

Livingstone's Africa, 1840–73

A remarkable man

With heavy hearts, Chuma, Susi, Magwara and Farjeli prepared the body for the first stage of its long journey back to England. As a final tribute to their great leader, they had decided to risk the dangerous and exacting trek to the coast with the corpse. They did not know that in his diaries the old man himself had expressed the wish to be buried under the 'still, still trees of Africa' where no one would disturb his bones.

For two weeks, and with utmost care, they had embalmed the body by rubbing salt into the skin and bathing the lips and hair with brandy. Daily they had baked the body under the burning heat of the mid-day sun; at night they had taken turns guarding it from hyenas and other predators. Then they had wrapped the corpse in a skin and enclosed it in a cylinder of bark. Finally, they had bound the package with sailcloth painted with tar which had been intended for the man's boat. When finished, they had fastened it to a long pole so that it could be carried.

Before the body had been embalmed, Farjeli, who had once worked for a doctor, cut out the dead man's heart and entrails. These were buried in a tin under a nearby huge mvule tree. Then, Jacob Wainwright, a freed slave who had been educated by missionaries in India and who had taken a European name as a tribute to them, read the burial service from the dead man's own prayer book. For ever, the heart of their great leader, their *Bwana mkubwa*, would remain in Africa, in the country to which he had devoted his life.

The group worked quickly and quietly, afraid that the nearby villagers would demand *hongo* if they knew a stranger had died there. *Hongo* was a levy, one which would have to be paid in kind and which would drastically reduce the stores that would be badly needed if they were to reach the coast successfully.

The body was that of Dr David Livingstone – a man who, in England, had become a legend in his own lifetime. For weeks before his death, Livingstone had been critically ill. Full of fever, unable to eat, almost blind and suffering from crippling internal bleeding, he and his loyal servants had struggled on against all odds as they journeyed south from Lake Tanganyika. All the time, Livingstone was becoming weaker, though no one realized that death was so close. On reaching the edge of the Bangweolo swamps some 350 miles (560 km) west of Lake Nyasa, Livingstone had become so ill that the servants decided to stop and build him a hut so that he could rest.

Then, late one night, Magwara discovered his leader kneeling motionless beside his bed as if deep in prayer. His sextant, chronometer, Bible and metal-backed notebook lay beside him. The body was almost cold. Livingstone had been dead some while.

David Livingstone died on the 1 May 1873, three weeks after his sixtieth birthday. On a tree nearby, Jacob Wainwright carved his initials and the date of his death. Only he carved 4 May. Somehow he had got the date wrong. But no matter, precise dates were never all that important in central Africa 130 years ago.

The cortège consisted of 80 men, ten of whom died on the journey. Transporting the body to the coast meant a 1,500-mile (2,400 km) trek on foot – a daunting enough task in itself without having to manhandle a corpse slung from a pole. The route took them over the Murthinga mountains, across arid bush and then through dense rainforest. Nineteenth-century Africa – the 'dark' continent as it was called – had no proper roads connecting the villages to make passage simple. The group knew it would be a gruelling task requiring them to struggle through the unforgiving country as best they could, fighting disease, hunger and thirst every inch of the way. Between the Bangweolo swamps and the coast they would have to cope not only with difficult country, but also with warring tribes, slave-traders and dangerous animals. The exhausting journey was to take them more than eight months to complete.

Five months after setting out, the cortège staggered into Tabora on the border between modern-day Tanzani and Kenya. There they met Lieutenant Cameron, another explorer and leader of one of the groups sent out to find Livingstone. He tried to persuade the party to bury the body there and then but he had not counted on their resolve to perform their final duty to their *Bwana*. Granting their wish, Cameron replenished their supplies and they continued their trek eastwards towards the shores of the Indian Ocean.

Eventually they arrived at Bagamoyo, a coastal town just north of Dar es Salaam. From there, Livingstone's body was shipped across the channel separating the mainland from Zanzibar island. In the port there, the body was loaded on to a British ship and the world-famous explorer began his last journey – back to England and to his final resting place.

EARLY DAYS

Who was this man who engendered such devotion from his African servants?

David Livingstone was born on 19 March 1813 at Blantyre near Glasgow. For someone who was to achieve such great international fame and recognition, he had an unpretentious background. His family of nine lived in a single room at the top of a tenement building, little more than 9 feet by 9 (8 m²), but he remained proud of his working-class origins and never resented the luxuries enjoyed by the wealthy. David, together with his two brothers and two sisters, had a strict religious upbringing which laid the basis of the Christian faith which, to his dying day, he never once disavowed. In his journals and letters, he acknowledged time and again that Christianity was the inspiration and driving force behind all his work. Whether or not one accepts his religious views, it is doubtful whether, without them, he could have overcome the immense obstacles, frustrations and problems which were to be his lot. Even in early life, the qualities which were to make him such an outstanding nineteenth-century figure soon began to emerge. These included his unremitting capacity for hard work, his all-consuming interest in every branch of literature and science and, of course, his complete devotion to the Christian faith.

Nineteenth-century Blantyre was a busy cotton-spinning and weaving town. David received his basic education at the local school. When he was ten, he went to work in a cotton mill where children as young as five worked. His job as a 'piecer' entailed walking between the reels of the spinning jennies and tying together the broken threads. It was tedious and dangerous work but David immediately showed his capacity for hard work, toiling from six in the morning till eight at night. With his first pay packet, he purchased a Latin primer. This he propped up on a loom at the mill, studying it as he passed between the machines repairing broken threads. The girl spinners amused themselves by taking pot-shots at it with bobbins, hoping to knock it flying. He was a voracious reader of any book available, from those of classical authors such as Virgil and Homer to ones on science, though novels never interested him. He also became a competent mathematician, learning skills which were to be invaluable in his later navigational and surveying work. He was ahead of his time in seeing no clash between science and religion – this to the chagrin of his father who believed in a literal interpretation of the Bible.

At age 13, he joined evening classes. These started as soon as he finished at the mill and lasted until ten; then he did two hours' homework before going to bed. In his little spare time, he scoured the countryside with his brothers looking for samples connected with his varied interests in botany, geology and zoology.

He was, truly, a nineteenth-century workaholic.

THE MISSIONARY CALL

When he was 20, his simple acceptance of Christianity became a passionate conviction and he began to give all his spare cash to missionary causes. He did not, however, think of becoming a missionary himself until he heard an appeal for medical missionaries to go to China. This became his ambition and he realized that, somehow or other, he had to qualify as a doctor. Training in medicine required attendance at Anderson's College Glasgow for two six-month sessions – the medical curriculum was not, of course, as extensive then as now. In those days, there were no grants or student loans; he financed himself by first studying for six months, then working in the mills for six months. He attended his first session during the winter of 1836–37. Being a demon for hard work, he combined medical studies with that of Greek and theology, seldom sleeping more than two or three hours a night.

He returned to the college at Glasgow for his second – and final – session in the winter of 1837–38. His savings from the mill were insufficient to cover the cost of his studies and he had to borrow money from his brother to see him through. He also applied to the LMS (i.e. the London Missionary Society, now the Council for World Mission) for appointment as a missionary. He chose the LMS as it was a very 'open-minded' organization, accepting applicants from a wide range of religious backgrounds. This appealed to Livingstone. He was interviewed by the society's directors in July 1838 and was selected for three-months' training at their missionary training school at Chipping Ongar. As Ongar was near London, he was able to advance his medical studies at the London hospitals.

He did not impress his tutors as a potential preacher. His final report criticized his hesitation in leading prayers, describing him as a complete failure in the pulpit. Fortunately for Livingstone, a member of the examining board successfully pleaded for him to have a second chance. A further report, in January 1839, was more favourable and he was 'formally accepted' by the society as a missionary.

In November 1840, Livingstone graduated as a Licentiate of the Faculty of Physicians and Surgeons of Glasgow, thus becoming a qualified doctor. In that month, he was also formally ordained. Livingstone was to spend the next 30 years of his life working, not in China but in Africa, and he was to die there.

✻ ✻ ✻ SUMMARY ✻ ✻ ✻

- David Livingstone, born 1813, had a strict religious upbringing.

- His first job was in a mill when aged ten. An avid reader, he taught himself Latin.

- He became passionately committed to Christianity at age 20.

- He studied medicine, then trained as a missionary.

- In November 1840, he was ordained and also qualified as a doctor.

- He spent his life preaching and exploring in Africa, earning a worldwide reputation.

- He died in 1873.

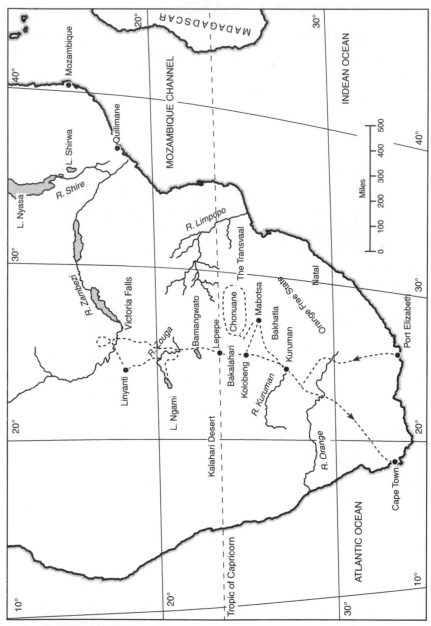

Livingstone's early journeys, 1841–52

The call of Africa, 1840–43

CHANGE OF PLAN

Livinstone's original ambition to work in China was thwarted by the Opium Wars caused by China's attempt to prevent the East India Company importing opium into China to earn money for the purchase of the increasing quantities of tea being demanded in England. The trade was having horrendous effects on Chinese addicts and creating immense social problems for the Chinese government. But it also generated huge profits for British businesses. The small British expeditionary force sent to China was quickly victorious. By the Treaty of Nanking, China was forced to legalize opium imports, to pay Britain sizeable compensation and cede her five Chinese ports. In retaliation, China prohibited the entry of missionaries, a restriction not lifted until 1858. The wars represent one of the darker sides of British imperialism.

As China was no longer a possibility, the LMS directors decided to send Livingstone to the West Indies. With typical single-mindedness, Livingstone objected, arguing there were enough missionaries there already. A chance meeting with **Dr Robert Moffat** proved to be a watershed in Livingstone's career. Moffat convinced him that Africa was the place to go and, thereafter, Livingstone wished to work nowhere else. Against a man with Livingstone's level of determination, the directors of the LMS stood no chance.

KEYWORDS

Dr Robert Moffat was a distinguished Scottish missionary and an able scholar who translated the whole Bible into Tswana. He worked tirelessly among African communities to improve methods of irrigation and agriculture. The LMS posted him to South Africa where he worked for 49 years, building up one of the foremost Protestant missionary centres at Kuruman (see Frontispiece) in central Africa. Kuruman was central to much of Livingstone's life and work. It was here that he met Dr Moffat's daughter whom he later married and where some of his children were born. He often sought shelter here.

OUTWARD BOUND

On 8 December 1840, Livingstone embarked on the *George* bound for Cape Town. It was to be an adventurous and useful journey. Livingstone persuaded the captain to teach him how to 'fix' a position by reference to the stars. The lessons often extended long into the cloudless nights as the ship nosed its way towards the South Atlantic. It provided Livingstone with skills essential to any explorer, enabling him to record the location of discoveries with a precision which won the admiration of geographers worldwide. They also proved vital when, many years later, he navigated his own boat – a lake steamer – across the Indian Ocean. Livingstone also used the time to teach himself the rudiments of the Dutch and Sechuana languages. He did not believe in wasting time.

In mid-Atlantic, gales broke the ship's fore-mast. This meant putting into Rio de Janeiro for repairs. It may seem strange that a ship bound for Africa should divert to South America, but a glance at a globe – as opposed to an atlas – will show that for a major part of the journey, Brazilian harbours are the nearest ports of call. Atlases usually draw lines of longitude parallel to one another (although they actually curve towards one another as they move away from the equator towards the poles). This distorts the impressions of areas and of distances. Also, there were very few West African ports capable of handling the work.

Whilst in Rio, Livingstone made a point of mixing with local people, all of whom were most kind to him and often would take no money for the meals they gave him. This showed his great natural ability to 'get on with the locals', a skill sadly lacking when dealing with his peers – he could be an extremely difficult man to work with. He was markedly unimpressed with the example set by Rio's European population who, it seemed to him, spent the majority of their time getting drunk.

Livingstone felt little empathy with the religious services held on board since the chaplain assumed that everyone was Christian, ignoring anyone who wasn't. Livingstone was further concerned at the amount of drunkenness and immorality among the sailors. The need to meet the social as well as religious problems of seamen came home to him as he tried, in a Rio hospital, to comfort a dying seaman who, when drunk, had been stabbed and robbed. This need has, of course, been largely met since by the growth of the Mission to Seafarers (formerly Missions to Seamen) movement which has established havens for mariners of all races and creeds in ports throughout the world.

ARRIVAL IN AFRICA

Livingstone arrived in Cape Town on 14 March 1841. He took lodgings with Dr and Mrs John Philip. Dr Philip was not a missionary but for many years had acted as the LMS's agent. He was a man who worked tirelessly for the good of native Africans and was instrumental in making their gross exploitation public knowledge. Livingstone developed a high regard for Dr Philip but his views were not universally accepted. Philip, who was responsible for the finance and general administration of the society's affairs in South Africa, was often autocratic when dealing with other missionaries and this caused him considerable unpopularity. Also he and Dr Moffat, that other great charismatic missionary whom Livingstone had met in London, were at loggerheads over many policy issues, particularly whether missions should expand into new areas. Moffat, as well as Livingstone, thought this the way forward but Philip considered that resources should be used for consolidating established missions. The rift between Philip and Moffat grew deeper over the years and ultimately sank to abysmal levels of personal animosity. There were, Livingstone considered, faults on both sides.

THE STATE OF THE CHURCH IN AFRICA

The disagreements between Philip and Moffat were only part of Livingstone's concern over the sad state of affairs existing within African churches. He was greatly disturbed by both the hostility between French and British missionaries and the extent to which those working north of the Orange River were at odds with those in the south. Even within each group, there were rival factions. In a letter home, he described the Church as being 'in a deplorable state … a house divided against itself'.

Livingstone also had grave reservations regarding the lifestyle and ambitions of many missionaries. He divided them into two groups – the *colonial side* who enjoyed a comfortable existence in the settled areas of the Cape, and the *native side* who were dedicated to the welfare of Africans and prepared to suffer the discomforts of life on distant stations. He made no secret of the fact that he thought there were far too many 'colonial side' missionaries and, with his customary forthrightness, told the LMS so.

JOURNEY TO KURUMAN – AND BEYOND

After a month with Dr Philip, Livingstone sailed to Port Elizabeth and from there travelled by ox wagon to Dr Moffat's mission station at Kuruman. Kuruman is situated in central Africa, a little south of present-day Botswana (formally Bechuanaland). It required a journey of well over 500 miles (800 km) through very difficult country with hills rising steeply to 3,000 feet (900 m) or more. No roads or tracks marked the path to this extremely remote area. Despite the painfully slow, lumbering journey which took ten weeks to complete, Livingstone recorded in his journal that he enjoyed every minute of it, developing a taste for travel he never lost. Throughout the journey, the scientist in him came to the fore. He carefully catalogued every type of tree he passed and collected samples of each type of rock.

Livingstone's one regret about the journey was that reading and study were difficult. But that did not stop him thinking. Even at that early stage of his career, he began to develop his ideas for expanding the work of missions through **native agents**, an idea strongly opposed by Dr Philip. Native agents were well-trained local converts who spoke the languages of the areas in

KEYWORDS

Native agent: a local African convert to Christianity prepared to preach and teach in outlying districts in his own language.

which they would serve. Also, Livingstone's letters and journal began to give the first hint of the importance of developing commerce between local tribes and Europeans. He saw this as the best way to improve the welfare of Africans – he was later to see it as fundamental in undermining the iniquitous slave trade, the extent of which he did not, as yet, appreciate. His letters also comment on how his medical skills were beginning to attract large numbers of local people and to increase their confidence in him. The link between preaching, education and medicine can be traced back to early Greece. It is interesting, as any assessment of the achievements of Christian missions in Africa must highlight their enormous contribution in providing hospitals and schools – both primary and secondary – throughout large parts of the African continent.

At that time, Kuruman was the most northerly missionary station in southern Africa. Beyond it stretched the harsh, arid and unexplored Kalahari desert. Livingstone arrived there in July 1841 expecting instructions to be waiting for him, but none had arrived. His only guidance was to wait at Kuruman for the return of Dr Moffat who continued to be delayed in England dealing with the publication of his translation of the New Testament. He did not return to Kuruman until 1843, more than a year after Livingstone's arrival there.

Livingstone had, however, been asked to investigate the possibilities of establishing new mission stations further north. Intent on making the best use of available time, he immediately set about planning his first journey into the **Interior** to assess the feasibility of establishing permanent mission stations in the unexplored regions. He was convinced that missionaries should be prepared to identify themselves with the natives, and to learn their languages in order to understand their thoughts and feelings. This was, of course, one of his root criticisms of the 'colonial side' missionaries in the south.

KEYWORD

The Interior was the common term used for the vast stretches of Africa which lay away from the immediate hinterland of the coast. Little was known of it in 1840 except that it was (mistakenly) believed to be mainly unpopulated desert.

In September 1841, he began an arduous 700-mile (1,100 km) circular journey, taking with him two African Christians. He hoped to establish them in suitable areas where they could preach and teach. He proposed to meet the costs of one of them personally. It is difficult today to appreciate the difficulties of travel in those days. Travelling by ox-wagon, the journey took three months. Oxen can draw heavy loads but are not the speediest of animals. What with having to cross swamps, ford rivers and cope with rough country densely covered with thick bush entangled with fallen trees, any party was lucky if it could cover three miles (five kilometres) in an hour. Many of the people he met had never seen a white man before. The trip convinced him that the recruitment of native agents who could teach as well as preach was the key to expansion.

SECOND JOURNEY FROM KURUMAN

In February 1842 Livingstone set out on his second journey from Kuruman, an expedition which was to result in him travelling more than 1,000 miles (1,600 km) by wagon and on foot. His objectives were to:

* fulfil a promise he had made to the northern people that he would return – throughout his life, Livingstone claimed he never broke a promise;

* acquire greater fluency in the Sechuana language;

* engage in direct evangelism assisted by native agents.

Livingstone left Kuruman with two converts and two drivers. For 12 days he travelled along the fringes of the unforgiving Kalahari desert to Bakhatla in the southern reaches of present-day Botswana. He then travelled north for a further 100 miles (160 km) to Lepepe, just north of the Tropic of Capricorn. With local villagers, he constructed an irrigation canal 500 feet (150 m) long, 3 feet (1 m) wide and 4 feet (1.2 m) deep. A small task today perhaps, but the equipment available to Livingstone and his volunteers was one spade; even that had no handle. It gave Livingstone the reputation of being a 'rainmaker' and something of a god – a reputation he found embarrassing, particularly when the rains failed. After a month, he set out again northwards for the town of Bamangwato.

The return journey took him within ten days' travel of Lake 'Ngami, but as exploration had yet to become his primary objective he did not divert from his planned route. He visited a number of tribes on the way including the Mashona whose language was markedly different from those he already knew. The Mashona were an industrious people who produced cotton, cloth, iron and copper goods, which he found encouraging. What he found less encouraging was that they had obtained guns by selling slaves to the Portuguese.

A nearby tribal chief asked Livingstone's advice whether he and his tribe should return to their lands further south after having been evicted by another tribe. Livingstone strongly advised against it but was ignored. The chief returned south. As Livingstone feared, the result was a blood-bath.

Livingstone arrived back at Kuruman in June 1842. It was to be a year before he received a letter from the LMS turning down his request to establish a network of native agents and suggesting that such matters should in future be decided by local committees. The society did, however, authorize him to establish a permanent station north of Kuruman. He thought a likely spot would be Mabotsa, just over 100 miles (160 km) further north.

In August 1843, he said goodbye to Dr Moffat and set off for Mabotsa.

* * *SUMMARY* * *

• The Opium Wars prevented Livingstone going to China as a medical missionary.

• As a result of meeting Dr Moffat, he decided to go to Africa instead.

• On the way, he learnt invaluable navigation skills and basic Sechuana and Dutch.

• At Cape Town, he lodged with Dr Philip but was disturbed by the internal dissent within the Church and between the missionaries. He became critical of the comfortable life style of many Cape missionaries.

• He travelled to Kuruman and between September 1841 and June 1842, undertook two journeys into the Interior. He was later appalled to find a local tribe selling slaves to the Portuguese in return for guns.

• Livingstone became convinced that 'native agents' were the key to expansion.

• In August 1843, Livingstone left Kuruman after (eventually) receiving approval from the LMS to establish a station at Mabotsa, but permission to train native agents was refused.

3 Life at Mabotsa, 1843–46

Livingstone located his first mission at Mabotsa, 200 miles (320 km) north of Kolobeng, near present-day Mafeking which, in 1899, was besieged by the Boers for 217 days and whose relief has gone down in history. Attractive and well wooded, Mabotsa had ample water and good supplies of iron ore in nearby hills. The local people, an industrious, agriculture-based community, welcomed Livingstone's arrival.

MAULED BY A LION

Livingstone spent the closing months of 1843 building a large mission hut but, in February 1844, a serious incident occurred. He was attacked by a lion. But for the resourcefulness and bravery of Mabalwe, one of his African teachers, he would not have survived. His left shoulder was badly mauled with several serious fractures to his arm. Asked later what his emotions were at the time, he said that the shock must have induced something of a stupor for he felt no pain. His only concern was wondering which part of him the lion would eat first. The wounds were later lanced and the bones reset without anaesthetic. The damage was such that he was unable, afterwards, to shoot from the shoulder and he adopted a technique of firing from the waist. It was from his descriptions of the wounds that his body was identified when returned to England after his death. Livingstone's inborn confidence in what he saw as God's great benevolence did not desert him even at that time. He later wrote to his father saying that nothing but praise was due to the Almighty for having saved him and that gratitude for his deliverance was the only sentiment everyone should feel.

BACK TO KURUMAN – AND MARRIAGE

Two months after the attack Livingstone had recovered sufficiently to return to Kuruman where he met the committee set up by the LMS. His differences with several members of it made relations very difficult and shows clearly just how much better he was at getting on with his followers than with his peers.

Dr Moffat had settled back at Kuruman before Livingstone's return and had brought with him his wife and Mary, their 23-year-old daughter. Livingstone had but recently been considering marriage, even thinking of advertising in the *Evangelical Magazine* – an unlikely dating agency one might think – for a suitable widow. However, Mary's appearance on the scene altered all that. She had many desirable qualities. Having been brought up in a missionary household, she knew full well the demands of such a life and, as well as being a competent teacher, she had certain qualities of tact and refinement which he himself patently lacked.

Records suggest there was little romance in their courtship. Livingstone seems to have approached the whole thing in a very matter of fact sort of way. When writing to the directors of the LMS, he claimed that he had married because 'various considerations' made him decide that such was his duty and that marriage would enable him to promote the 'Divine glory' that much better. However, too much should not be read into the apparent unemotional relationship. Although he usually signed letters to his wife (and later even to his children) with just an initial and his surname, the letters themselves were full of warmth and love, and this was reciprocated in her communications to him.

The couple married in January 1845. It was to be a hard life for Mary. She bore her husband six children, one dying when only six weeks old. Her lot involved long and strenuous journeys, through extremely unhealthy areas, which she was hardly fit to make. She had to suffer frequent separations from her husband who always saw his work as a missionary, and later as an explorer, as the prime purpose of his life. His family never occupied more than second place in his list of priorities. At no time did Livingstone reproach himself for, or accept any criticism of, his chosen way of life or the pressures to which he subjected his family. Mary remained a loyal and dutiful wife to him to the day she died, never once complaining. Her death left Livingstone heartbroken.

Livingstone continued to regard the appointment of native agents as crucial, and he saw Mabotsa as a possible training centre. His views, however, continued to meet with strong opposition. Some thought the idea was premature; others that he was simply angling for a comfortable principalship of a training seminary. The irony is that, had his suggestions been accepted, he might never have undertaken his explorations or have become so instrumental in fighting slavery.

THE MOVES TO CHONUANE AND TO KOLOBENG

Livingstone worked happily at Mabotsa for a couple of years. When building a house there, he dropped some heavy building materials and nearly ruined the repair to his fractured arm by instinctively grabbing at them. The arm healed successfully after being bandaged by Baba, a helper. Two years later, the unfortunate Baba was ripped to pieces by a rhinoceros.

In 1846, serious differences arose between Livingstone and another missionary. The animosity became so great that Livingstone decided to move on and establish a new missionary station at Chonuane, 40 miles (64 km) further north. He was there hardly long enough to build his second house when, because of water shortages, he decided to move even further north, this time to Kolobeng where he began building his third house. This one was intended as a temporary structure to be replaced by a permanent home a year later. The great reputation which Livingstone now began to enjoy as a preacher would have astounded those who had been so critical of him at Chipping Ongar. He had learnt to adapt his style to his listeners and to address them in a simple, conversational way which captured their attention.

SOME PROBLEMS

In his ministries at Chonuane and Kolobeng, Livingstone encountered two major problems. The first was the practice of polygyny and the Church's insistence – despite little biblical authority – on monogamy. The problem came to a head with the conversion of a tribal chief at Chonuane. He was so keen to adopt the Christian way of life that, after his baptism, he 'sent away' his surplus wives. The Church's rule caused widespread resentment and lost Livingstone many potential converts. Although he recognized the rule, Livingstone doubted its advisability in the African situation – he once wrote 'all friends of divorced wives become the opponents of our religion'. He did, however, concede that another chief who had 48 wives, 20 children, and was still only 20 years old, was taking things a bit far.

In many ways, polygyny was – and still is – part of the fabric of African society. Quite apart from the prestige that several wives give a husband (particularly important to chiefs and village elders), wives undertake much heavy work. In addition to cleaning, washing and cooking, they are responsible for gathering fuel from the woods and fetching water, often from distant wells.

The second problem Livingstone had to face centred around the **Boers**. From Chonuane, Livingstone made two journeys east to investigate the possibility of establishing local agents. This would require the goodwill of Boers who did not share Livingstone's commitment to the welfare and development of the native African population. They saw themselves as a Christian elect with a divine right to rule, believing the Africans were there to serve them. The Boers controlled all the wells, demanded unpaid labour from the local Africans and often forcibly seized their cattle. They used Africans as front-line troops in battle so that they took the brunt of the enemy fire. Livingstone found that

KEY FACT

Polygyny is the practice of one husband having several wives. It is common among a number of African tribes and is permitted by some religions. Polyandry, the practice of one wife having several husbands, is occasionally found in societies that practise female infanticide.

Polygamy is a general term covering both polygyny and polyandry.

KEYWORD

The **Boers** (now usually called *Afrikaners*) are of Dutch-Huguenot descent. In 1652, they settled in Africa after the Dutch East India Company set up a shipping station at the Cape of Good Hope. The Cape became a British possession in 1806 as a result of the Napoleonic Wars. The Boers quickly became disillusioned with British rule, particularly over borders and the freeing of slaves. This led to the 'Great Trek' to southern Natal, 1835–43. The Boers developed their own variant of the Dutch language known as Afrikaans.

the Africans were unprotected by any laws and suffered 'the most flagrant injustice (with) the most foul massacres (being) justified on the grounds that they were necessary to subdue the troublesome tendencies of the people'.

The Boers disliked intensely the way Livingstone identified with the African population and made many complaints about his activities to the colonial government. Their attitude towards him varied from one of little co-operation to one of outright hostility. Boer resistance was so strong that Livingstone realized that there was no chance of placing native agents anywhere east of Kolobeng and that he would therefore have to investigate the possibilities westwards.

* * *SUMMARY* * *

- At Mabotsa, his first mission station, Livingstone was badly mauled by a lion. Whilst recuperating at Kuruman, he met and subsequently married Mary Moffat.

- Following personality clashes with another missionary at Mabotsa, Livingstone moved north to Chonuane. Conditions there proved unsuitable so he moved even further north to Kolobeng.

- Livingstone found the Church's insistence on monogamy greatly restricted the number of converts.

- He had to face considerable resistance from the Boers who treated the Africans with harsh repression.

- Livingstone realized that he would have to search westwards for suitable locations for further expansion.

Lake 'Ngami – and beyond, 1846–52

4

DISCOVERY OF LAKE 'NGAMI

Kolobeng proved no better as a missionary station than Chonuane. The water supply was even more limited and the majority of the population was absent for long periods – the men were forced to travel far and wide hunting for food and the women were away searching for locusts. This meant small attendances at both church and school, and very limited scope for missionary work. Consequently, Livingstone happily agreed when a local chief suggested he should travel northwards to explore **Lake 'Ngami** – a lake shrouded in mystery which had, despite several earlier attempts, never been reached by a white man.

Livingstone's main interest was not so much with the lake as with his conviction that, somewhere north of Kolobeng, there must lie a region suitable for European settlement which would be ideal, not only for a mission station, but also as a commercial centre. He also became increasingly convinced that a route existed, either to the east or the west, which could provide access to the region for commerce and immigration. Discovery of such a route became his prime objective. The wish was instrumental in turning him from missionary work to exploration.

KEYWORD

Lake 'Ngami (20.30S 22.46E) is a shallow, marshy lake on the southern edge of the much larger Okavango marsh. It extends over 10,400 square kilometres and dries up during the dry season. The area is extremely rich in bird-life – and mosquitoes.

Being so shallow, the lake is highly susceptible to changes in climate and rainfall. The 1965–66 drought dried the lake up completely resulting in immense hardship for the local owners of thousands of cattle. The return of the rains partially replenished the lake, but it remains much smaller than when Livingstone first saw it. Global warming and increased demands for water are expected to increase the shrinkage.

Livingstone's party left Kolobeng on 1 June 1849. After travelling for several days without water, they reached Serotle. They then had to cross the north-east corner of the Kalahari desert and face a journey of 70 miles (113 km) without a watering place. The heat was such that the party could only travel a few hours after sunrise and a few before sunset, making no more than six miles (10 km) a day. The terrain became so barren that even the guides were lost. Eventually, a bushwoman – who had initially been mistaken for a lion – led them to a spring eight miles (13 km) away. By early July, the party had travelled 300 miles (480 km). They still had 300 miles to go. After a few days, they sighted the Zouga River with a small village on its far bank. The friendly and peace-loving people spoke a language unfamiliar to Livingstone, but he managed to ascertain that the Zouga led to the lake for which he was searching.

The Zouga proved to have many tributaries and Livingstone began to have high hopes that he had discovered the 'highway' into Central Africa that he so desperately desired. After following the river for 12 days, he arrived at the lake which at first appeared to be 'an unbounded sheet of water' – unfortunately, it proved to be only a marshy swamp, a massive breeding ground for disease, mosquitoes and, of course, **malaria**. Livingstone waded into the lake for half a mile but found it no more than waist deep. Leeches forced his withdrawal.

In Livingstone's day, the connection between malaria and its transmission by female mosquitoes was unknown. Its treatment was known before its cause. Quinine, obtained from the bark of cinchona trees, was used by Jesuit priests in Peru as early as 1700. Livingstone compounded pills from quinine and other elements and this proved reasonably effective in

KEYWORD

Malaria, one of the world's top six major killers, is responsible for over a million deaths annually. Attempts to eradicate it with DDT have failed as mosquitoes have a natural ability to develop resistance to pesticides. Malaria is now spreading to new areas. Anyone travelling to a malarial region should, in their own interest, follow medical advice regarding the latest prophylactics (drugs which *prevent* infection) well *before* departure and continue them for the prescribed period *after* return as the malarial parasite can lie dormant in the blood for some while.

controlling, though not preventing, the condition. Unfortunately, quinine has adverse side effects involving hearing and sight loss, both of which affected Livingstone. He describes the 'dreadful' mosquito bites from which his children suffered with not a single 'square half-inch of their little bodies' unaffected. He also recounts how mosquitoes made sleep impossible. It is no wonder that his two elder children and others in the party became so ill with malaria that they pressed Livingstone to return home, but he continued with plans to drive on further north, still convinced that somewhere there was country suitable for Europeans. He finally had to abandon all hope when the local chief refused him the necessary guides. He suspected that Livingstone's intention was to arm the northern people, making them dangerous neighbours. Livingstone was unable to convince him otherwise. Nevertheless, the discovery of the lake was considered an exceptional achievement and the LMS awarded him 25 guineas – not an insignificant sum in those days.

A SECOND PROBE NORTH

Livingstone set out again the following year still hoping to probe the territory north of the lake. He insisted on taking with him his wife, who was in poor health and hardly fit for such a journey, and his children. This he did against the strongest pleas from Dr and Mrs Moffat who, of all people, knew the dangers associated with lack of water, the mosquito scourge and the ever-present catalogue of fevers endemic in nineteenth-century Africa. It was, in fact, the fever coupled with the constant tsetse fly attacks on his oxen, that caused Livingstone to abandon his attempt. He returned to Kolobeng with a wife who was heavily pregnant.

Why did Livingstone take his family on such a journey? Was it his unwillingness to be separated from them if it could possibly be avoided? Was it because he considered the help of his wife as essential to his missionary work? Was it his sublime belief in Providence and that the Almighty would look after them? Or was it just a selfish inconsideration for his family and a blind belief in the rightfulness of his mission? All of these reasons have been suggested.

SAD EVENTS

Back at Kolobeng, there occurred one of the saddest events in Livingstone's life. Shortly after reaching the station, his wife gave birth to their fourth child, a little girl. The child only lived six weeks, dying a traumatic death from an epidemic sweeping the area at the time. Livingstone's devastation at the loss was matched only by his grief at the death of his wife several years later.

This was not the end of his troubles. Mary Livingstone's pregnancy left her with paralysis of the right side of her face, arm and leg. Livingstone himself was also suffering from a badly infected uvula at the back of his throat. He refused to leave his wife and go to the Cape for treatment. Instead, he tried to persuade Dr Moffat, his father-in-law, to operate under his (Livingstone's) guidance. Moffat, it must be understood, was a theologian, not a medical man. At the last minute, Moffat lost his nerve and could not plunge the home-made instruments into Livingstone's throat.

ANOTHER ATTEMPT – AND ANOTHER DISCOVERY

Undeterred, Livingstone made a third attempt at the journey in April 1851. He wanted to reach the lands governed by an African chief named Sebituane, some 200 miles (320 km) north of Lake 'Ngami. He again took his family with him despite the difficulties and criticisms he had met with on the previous trip. It was also against the strongest pleas from the Moffats.

It was not an easy journey. Among other problems, the desert was drier than ever. Suffering the scorching desert heat, the party were several days without water and the well-being of the children became a serious concern. In his journal, he wrote perceptively 'no one knows the value of water until he is deprived of it'. One can ask which of us, today, really appreciates that which we have at the turn of a tap?

Sebituane made Livingstone very welcome; all went well until a difficult situation arose. Sebituane became seriously ill with inflammation of the lungs. As Sebituane approached death, Livingstone feared that if he offered treatment and it was unsuccessful, villagers might accuse him of causing their chief's death. Livingstone compromised. He said a few words of comfort and commended the man's soul to God.

Livingstone gave up hope of establishing a settlement in the area and decided to return to Kolobeng – but this was not before he discovered a great river, then called the Seshéke, whose existence had previously been unknown. It was later found to be part of the upper reaches of the Zambezi. He also heard stories of rapids in one direction, and of magnificent waterfalls in the other, but it was to be some years before he found those waterfalls.

Livingstone's party set off homeward on 13 August 1851 by ox-wagon. Whilst on trek his fifth child, a son, was born. A short while later, one of his other sons became very ill – probably with malaria. The lad had three successive attacks but fortunately survived.

When he arrived back at Kolobeng, Livingstone found the mission station had been deserted. He moved on to Kuruman and, after a short stay, he and his family travelled to Cape Town, arriving there in March 1852. He also received disturbing news that the tribe he had so recently been living with had resorted to slave-trading in order to obtain arms. Eight boys, captured from other tribes, had been traded for eight old muskets; a further 30 captives had been exchanged for three guns. These and other similar examples convinced Livingstone of the desperate need to develop trade with European manufactured produce (hopefully not guns) being exchanged for African ivory (this was before the days of the embargo on the export of ivory). Take away the need to trade in slaves and the slave trade would, he felt, disappear. The key was to find a route between the Interior and either the east or west coast.

With this conviction now firmly fixed in his mind, missionary work began to take second place to exploration.

THE CAFFRE WARS

Livingstone arrived back in Cape Town to find that the **Caffre Wars** had flared up again and feelings were running high throughout the Cape. Missionaries, anyone connected with the missionaries and, indeed, all those sympathetic towards Africans, were considered grossly unpatriotic. Livingstone, who was disgusted at the treatment of the Xhosa people by the white forces and the blundering of the British authorities, found himself regarded with considerable distrust.

The initial skirmishes between the Boers and the Xhosa had arisen from problems connected with cattle-trading and with Xhosa resentment at European penetration of their lands. In 1818, Britain joined forces with the Boers. The subsequent delineation of the territorial boundaries increased tension and fighting again broke out in 1834–35. Natal was then partly occupied by the British but the following year it was annexed without resistance by the Boers. Following an appeal by the Africans against the Boers' oppressive administration, Natal was reoccupied by the British in 1844. Resentment over the partial annexations by the British led to more fighting which resulted in further defeats of the Xhosa in 1853, the year following Livingstone's return. Unfortunately, that was not the end of the matter. In 1857, the Xhosa slaughtered all their cattle in mass defiance. This led to widespread starvation which undermined any effective resistance by them until 1887 when the final battles – and final annexations – took place.

> **KEYWORD**
>
> Caffre Wars (sometimes called Kaffir or Kaffr Wars, but properly termed Cape Frontier Wars) consisted of intermittent fighting over the period 1791–1891, between Cape Colonists and the Xhosa people of the Eastern Cape, and ended with the annexation of the Xhosa territories and their incorporation into the British-controlled Cape Colony. It was the most prolonged of all struggles against European intervention.

RETURN OF MRS LIVINGSTONE AND THE CHILDREN TO ENGLAND

Livingstone had other problems on his mind, particularly the welfare of his wife and children. He eventually but reluctantly decided to send them back to England and they left the Cape in April 1852. Livingstone's throat condition, which had caused him considerable difficulty in preaching, had continued to trouble him. He used his stay in the Cape to have the diseased uvula removed and also to take lessons from the Astronomer Royal in lunar observation.

Two months after his family's departure, Livingstone set out again for Kuruman.

* * *SUMMARY* * *

- After finding Kolobeng unsuitable, Livingstone agreed to search for Lake 'Ngami.

- The first attempt was abandoned after being refused guides. Fever caused the failure of the second attempt.

- Shortly after their return to Kolobeng, the Livingstones lost their newly born daughter. The condition of Livingstone's badly infected throat had become serious and his wife suffered partial paralysis post-natally.

- The third attempt was undermined by the death of the local chief. The unsettled future of the area made it difficult to remain there so Livingstone decided to return to Kolobeng.

- During the journey, Livingstone discovered a river whose existence was previously unknown.

- He found the mission centre at Kolobeng deserted so he returned to Kuruman and after a short stay, went on to Cape Town, arriving there in March 1852.

- News that the Africans with whom he had been staying had been engaged in trading slaves for guns made him keener than ever to develop legitimate commerce in the region.

- Back in Cape Town, Livingstone found the Caffre Wars had made missionaries and African sympathizers very unpopular.

- Reluctantly, he sent his family back to England.

5 Coast to coast, 1852–56

RETURN OF THE INTERIOR

Progress back to the Interior was delayed by a number of difficulties, including a broken wheel on the over-loaded wagon. Livingstone eventually reached Kuruman in August 1852 at the same time – though he did not know it – that Kolobeng was being razed to the ground by a Boer commando unit. They killed and pillaged, stealing furniture and cattle, and taking captive most of the local population. Later, in a letter home, Livingstone pointed to the fundamental clash in their philosophies. *They* (the Boers) were determined to close the country down: *he* was determined to open it up – or perish in the attempt.

Shortly after Christmas Livingstone left Kuruman for Kolobeng. He had wanted to see the destruction for himself and to visit his daughter's grave, but he heard the Boers were out to 'get him' so he bypassed the town to the west. He pressed on through Sebituane's territory and arrived at **Linyanti** in June 1853. He continued northwards following the course of what is now known to be the Zambezi, still hoping to find an area suitable for European settlement. On the

KEYWORD

Linyanti (18.10S 24.10E) is on the northern border of present-day Botswana, 200 miles (320 km) north-east of Lake 'Ngami. Linyanti was the centre for several of Livingstone's journeys.

way, he encountered a man called Mpepe, Sebituane's half-brother and rival. A supporter of the slave trade, he had tried three times to kill Sebituane. He was captured and killed by some of Sebituane's countrymen who were travelling with Livingstone. Shortly afterwards, they also met Mpepe's father and another headman, both of whom were known supporters of Mpepe's plan. They were axed to pieces and fed to the crocodiles. Such was the way of life in Africa.

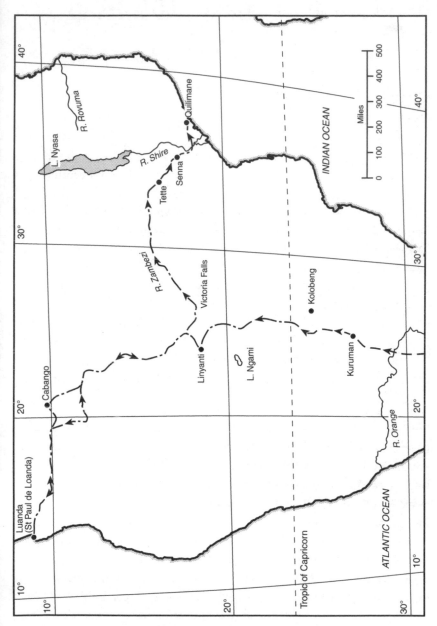

Livingstone's coast-to-coast expeditions, 1852–6

Unable to find a healthy area, Livingstone changed his plans and, hoping to find a direct route to the coast, struck out westwards but soon realized he was travelling in the wake of a Portuguese slave-trader. All villagers along the route had become fearful of any European. He therefore returned to Linyanti, deciding instead to head for Sao Paula de Loanda (now usually called **Luanda**) on the west coast of present-day Angola, 3,000 miles (4,800 km) from Linyanti.

KEYWORD

Luanda (8.58S 13.9E) is situated on the Atlantic coast of northern Angola and is now the country's capital. Founded in 1576 by the Portuguese, it became an administrative centre in 1627 and a major outlet for the slave trade to Brazil.

The journals that Livingstone assiduously kept throughout his life give a much more intimate picture of his thoughts and impressions at this time than either the formal reports he sent back to England or the books he later wrote. In his journal, he describes as 'indescribably vile' the pagan practices common among most tribes, particularly the heartless cruelty and infanticide; also the systematic and barbaric murder, plunder and oppression of peoples from other tribes. However, despite their paganism, there was widespread belief in a 'supreme being', though it was very much a god to be feared rather than one to be loved. He found that most tribal people accepted there would be an after-life whilst many believed in reincarnation.

On a more personal note, he comments on his frustration when, after preaching to attentive congregations of perhaps a thousand, his listeners would immediately return to their heathen rituals. He was appalled by the nakedness of the women yet he writes, with a note of unexpected elitism – almost sexism – for a missionary, that he had 'not met with a beautiful woman among the black people … a few who might be called passable (but) none at all to be compared (with) English servant girls.' He comments that he had heard of some 'beauties' among the Caffres, but he himself had not seen them. 'I cannot' he notes with a trace of what today might be interpreted as racism, 'conceive of any European being captivated by them.' He concluded that civilization alone 'produces beauty'.

Above all else, it was the slave trade that revolted him. Evidence of it was apparent everywhere, from the wanton killing and burning of crops and homes in the villages attacked, to the lines of chained men, women and children who were forced to trudge their miserable way to the coast. Despite Wilberforce's success in closing down the North Atlantic routes, slavery had continued to expand in Central Africa. It was still the 'open sore' of Africa. Livingstone could see no future for Christian missions, nor indeed for civilization, in the continent until the evil had been completely eradicated.

KEY FACT

It is not always appreciated that more slaves were taken from Central and East Africa than from West Africa. It is estimated that some ten million were exported from West Africa, whereas some 18 million were taken from Central and East Africa.

Livingstone took 27 men with him on his trek to Luanda, which was by far the most dangerous journey he had ever made. No European had ever travelled that way before and, being very short of stores, he found it difficult to placate the angry tribes he met en route. Thieves stole food and medicines soon after the start of the journey and, hit by successive bouts of fever, dysentery and severe depression, his health declined rapidly. The heavy rains and the constant need to wade through streams and swamps meant he was continuously wet. His chronic throat infection returned and the plagues of mosquitoes remained a constant irritation.

Livingstone arrived in Luanda on 31 May 1854, nearly seven months after finally leaving Linyanti, and was received by Edmund Gabriel, the British Commissioner. He found that lying in a proper bed after months of sleeping with the ground as his mattress and the sky his mantle, was sheer luxury.

The expedition had been outstanding because it was:

* the first journey of its kind – and the precursor of many;

* achieved with hardly any preparation and with totally inadequate equipment and provisions;
* undertaken at the worst time of the year – despite constant poor visibility, Livingstone charted the route and recorded his scientific observations with amazing accuracy;
* met with so much hostility *en route*;
* made with no official backing.

Livingstone was a sick man before he started the journey. He was half-dead from fever and starvation when he arrived – so sick that he could not pronounce his name. He was later awarded the Royal Geographical Society's Gold Medal – its highest honour – for his outstanding scientific work during the journey. The Astronomer Royal described him as 'having done more for the happiness of mankind than had been done by all (previous) African travellers put together'.

Livingstone remained in Luanda until September making many friends among the British naval officers whose work in suppressing the West Coast slave trade he so greatly admired. Although urged to return to England on a naval ship, he refused – despite his great wish to see his family – because he had promised his bearers that he would return them to their homes. The only way to do that was to travel with them; there was no way Livingstone was prepared to renege on a promise. In addition, he had still not accomplished his immediate task of finding a route to the coast. For a number of reasons, the west coast route was unsatisfactory. Therefore, a route east had to be found. His decision to remain was indeed fortuitous. The *Forerunner*, the naval ship on which he had been offered a passage, sank off Madeira in a storm. Only one person survived.

RETURN TO LINYANTI
The journey back to Linyanti was fraught with the usual struggles against malaria, dysentery and tribal opposition. In addition, Livingstone suffered rheumatic fever and severe internal bleeding of the colon – a

complaint which was to plague him for the rest of his life. He also had to battle against the monsoons. 'We were soaked if we went on; sodden if we stood still' he wrote. Anyone who has experienced the rains in Africa will know exactly what he meant. Despite his tribulations, he remained impressed, as he had been on his outward journey, by the fabulous beauty, richness and potential productivity of the land – and this in an area which previously had been considered just one vast, arid desert. The immense shame was the blight which the Portuguese, with their massive involvement in the slave trade, cast over the whole area.

It took Livingstone ten months, until July 1855, to reach Linyanti, the home of his bearers. He had managed the entire round trip, despite its immense dangers and risks, without losing one of them.

LOOKING EAST
There were several possible routes east. Livingstone chose the Zambezi option. It was the most difficult one and populated by extremely savage tribes, but it offered the most likely way through to the Indian Ocean. This time, his party consisted of 114 men. He had not travelled far from Linyanti when he stumbled on one of the most outstanding natural wonders of the world. It was the stupendous waterfalls which no European had ever seen – or even knew about. The local African name for them was *Mosi-oa-tun-ya* – the 'smoke which sounds'. Livingstone called them the Victoria Falls after the Queen he so admired. It was one of the only two times he used a European word to describe a location – the other was the Murchison Cataracts on the River Shiré, much later in his explorations. The Zambezi, 1,800 yards (1,620 m) broad at this point, tumbled over a deep fissure in the rocks some 80 feet (24 m) wide and 320 feet (98 m) deep – twice the fall of Niagara – and disappeared into vast clouds of spray. The raging, hissing water then zigzagged its way over and around rocks for more than 30 miles (48 km). On each side of the gorge, huge verdant tablelands spread out – country which provided excellent prospects for both missionary and commercial settlement. Visitors today, who have doubtless seen pictures of the falls, have some

idea what to expect, still find them breathtaking. Livingstone described the view as 'scenes so lovely (they) must have been gazed upon by angels in their flight'. It is difficult to imagine what the vista must have meant to someone stumbling upon them unexpectedly and with no pre-knowledge.

But the journey was far from over. It had, in fact, only just started. Livingstone's party fought on, mile after mile, struggling against fever, bad food, insufficient medicines, exhausting heat and toil, and suffering continual drenchings from the rains. Livingstone continued his scientific observations, recording that, despite the prevalence of fever, other medical conditions such as tuberculosis, cholera and cancer, seemed absent. This is surprising, since these conditions have since become recognized as major problems in Africa. It is possible that they were present but were written off as 'fever'. Livingstone identified many cases of sleeping sickness in animals (*tsetse morsitans*), but not one of the human form of the same disease (*tsetse trypanosoma*). However, it is questionable whether he was able to make accurate assessments of the illnesses as he struggled through bush and swamp.

Livingstone reached the Portuguese settlement of **Tette**, about 300 miles (480 km) from the coast, in March 1856, remaining there about six weeks. He was able to catch up on world news including the fall of Sevastopol and the end of the Crimea War. During this time, he wrote numerous letters to many influential people including the King of Portugal, pointing out the region's agricultural potential for such crops as wheat, wax, coffee, cotton, sugar, oil, honey and millet, for sheep-rearing and the production of iron. In view of the way African countries later developed and their emergence as world producers of staple agricultural commodities of the type Livingstone suggested, one can only acclaim the perceptiveness of his foresight.

KEYWORD

Tette (or Tete – 16.13S, 33.33E) is in west central Mozambique on the Zambezi. By the seventeenth century under Portuguese influence, it had become an important market for gold and ivory. Livingstone often used the harbour on his Zambezi expeditions.

From Tette, he travelled 100 miles (160 km) downriver to Senna and, from there, by boat to **Quilimane**. a major port situated 100 miles north of where the Zambezi delta pours its waters into the Indian Ocean. His arrival there was dogged by bad news. The Captain, Lieutenant and five crewmen of HMS *Dart*, under orders to transport him back to England, had drowned whilst attempting to approach Quilimane. Then he heard of the drowning in Canada of his nephew. To cap this, he received a terse letter from the LMS refusing to support any further activity not directly concerned with mission work. This was a bitter blow as Livingstone remained convinced that preaching, conversion and exploration were inextricably intertwined and that missionary success was dependent upon European settlement. Although the society changed its attitude later, the damage had been done. Determined to continue his work in the way he was convinced it should be done, Livingstone resigned from the society.

KEYWORD

Quilimane (or Quelimane – 17.53S, 36.58E), situated at the mouth of the Rio dos Bon Sinais River, is one of the oldest Portuguese settlements. Founded in 1544, it had a flourishing slave market throughout the eighteenth and nineteenth centuries. Used as a port by the Zambezi expeditions, the sandbars at its mouth seriously hindered navigation. It now boasts the world's largest coconut plantation (20,230 hectares).

The letter was not the end of the bad news. On the voyage back to England aboard the brig *Frolic*, his devoted personal servant Sekwebu became mentally confused and committed suicide. Then, at Cairo, Livingstone heard that his father had died. Finally, as his ship sailed across the Bay of Tunis, she was seriously damaged in a violent gale and almost lost. She limped into Marseilles and Livingstone, together with the other passengers, returned to England via Paris and Dover. This was unfortunate – Mrs Livingstone was waiting for him at Southampton.

✳ ✳ ✳ SUMMARY ✳ ✳ ✳

● Livingstone returned to Kuruman in August 1852 and later decided to travel to Kolobeng.

● Hearing that the Boers had ransacked Kolobeng, he moved on to Linyanti, deciding to look for a route westwards.

● After a long and dangerous journey he reached Luanda. The evils of the slave trade continued to dominate his thoughts.

● Despite serious health problems, Livingstone guided his men back to Linyanti, then set out in search of a route to the east – and discovered Victoria Falls. He struggled on to Tette, then to Quilimane where he embarked for England.

Home – and back again, 1856–60

6

RETURN TO ENGLAND

Those who knew Mary Livingstone in Africa may have had difficulty in recognizing her on her husband's return. She had experienced great difficulty in relating to the Livingstone family and received precious little help from the LMS. The strain of having no permanent home, the deep anxiety concerning her husband's welfare during the long periods without news, her solitude and the pressures of looking after a family of four on her own with little money, had all taken their toll and seriously affected her health. But there is no doubt that her love and admiration for him were undiminished; a poem she wrote shortly before his return amply illustrates that.

A hundred thousand welcomes and it's time for you to come
From the far off land of the foreigner, to your country and your home.
Oh, long as we were parted, ever since you went away,
I never passed a dreamless night, or knew an easy day.

Do you think I would reproach you with the sorrows that I bore?
Since the sorrow is all over, now I have you here once more,
And there's nothing but the gladness, and the love within my heart,
And the hope so sweet and certain that again we'll never part.

A hundred thousand welcomes! how my heart is gushing o'er
With the love and joy and wonder thus to see your face once more.
How did I live without you these long long years of woe?
It seems as if 'twould kill me to be parted from you now.

You'll never part me, darling, there's a promise in your eye;
I may tend you while I'm living, you will watch me when I die;
And if death but kindly lead me to the blessed home on high,
What a hundred thousand welcomes will await you in the sky.

(Mary Livingstone's poem written to welcome her husband home)

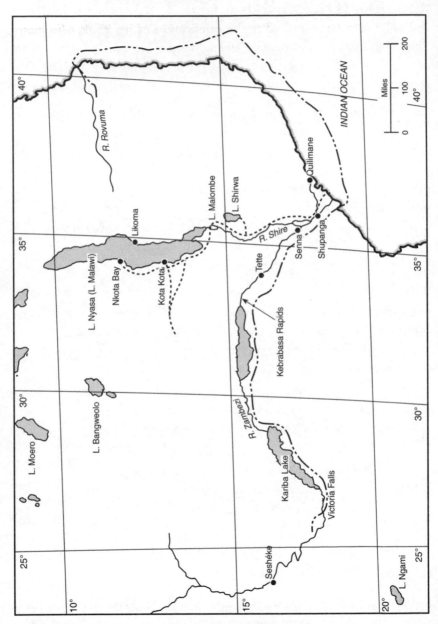

Livingstone's Zambezi and Rovuma expeditions, 1858–63

In December 1856, 15 years after his departure, Livingstone arrived back in England to fame and, after the publication of his book *Missionary Travels and Researches in South Africa*, fortune. He donated a large part of the proceeds to 'good causes'. In great demand as a speaker and lecturer, he attended meetings throughout the country including an address to the Royal Geographical Society convened in his honour. His listeners were amazed by his assessment of the potential riches of Africa. He caused a revolution in their understanding, not only of the country, but also of its people. He countered the many misleading newspaper reports of the Caffre Wars which had given the impression that all Africans were brutish, ferocious and ignorant. Livingstone gave details of Africa's climate and geological structure, its flora and fauna, its endemic diseases and which areas were healthy. He reported the exact location of numerous previously unknown hills, lakes and rivers. His talks excited the imagination of young missionaries, giving considerable impetus to their recruitment. Above all else, he opened people's eyes to the horrors of the massive amount of slave-trading that still existed in Central and East Africa.

For his work, Livingstone was awarded many honorary degrees and elected a Fellow of the Royal Society. He was granted audiences with the Prince Consort and then with the Queen herself, and was made a Freeman of the City of London.

Despite the hardships he had endured, his commitment to exploration remained. 'I go back to Africa' he announced in a speech at Cambridge, 'to make an open path for commerce and Christianity'. Despite his popularity, some critics saw his ambitions as contrary to missionary work and its ideals. The LMS, however, modified its previous letter and offered to allow him to return to Africa and continue to work as he saw fit, but Livingstone refused their entreaties, concerned he would still be encumbered with onerous restrictions.

Livingstone published his book in November 1857. Finding writing such a tiresome task, he swore never to write another. The book had to be completed very much 'against the clock' because of the danger that other authors would pirate his experiences. This gave precious little time to organize, shape, plan and revise it. The chapters were written 'as they dropped from the pen.' Nevertheless, the book was an instant best-seller.

BACK TO AFRICA – THE ZAMBEZI EXPEDITION

In February 1858, the Foreign Secretary invited Livingstone to lead a new expedition to explore the Zambezi. Its purpose was to investigate the navigability of the Zambezi up to the Kebrabasa Rapids, 100 miles (160 km) upriver from Tette, and to survey the network of tributaries branching off the main stream. The expedition was to occupy him for the next six years.

A shallow-draught, wood-burning paddle steamer, the *Ma-Robert*, was specially built at Birkenhead for the expedition. She was 75 feet (23 m) long with an 8-foot (2.5 m) beam and could carry 36 men plus 12 tons of freight. The boat was prefabricated in sections to allow assembly after transportation.

A varied collection of experts went with Livingstone, including a naval commander, a botanist and physician, a mining geologist, a marine engineer and an artist and storekeeper. Charles Livingstone, brother of Dr Livingstone, also went along as general assistant and secretary. None of them had any real experience of Africa.

Since the expedition would have to travel through their territory, Portuguese agreement was needed. Livingstone intended travelling to Lisbon to obtain the approval from the Portuguese Ambassador to England, whom he knew well, but yellow fever was raging there at the time. As time was short, the visit had to be cancelled. Nevertheless, Livingstone received from him a number of letters addressed to the local Portuguese governors, requesting their co-operation.

Livingstone's expedition and the dismantled paddle steamer sailed from Liverpool on 10 March 1858 aboard HM Colonial Steamer, *Pearl*. Despite Mrs Livingstone's weak condition, she and their youngest son Oswald accompanied them. Fair winds and good weather meant the ship made good time and reached Sierra Leone in 14 days but, after leaving Sierra Leone, the health of Mrs Livingstone, pregnant with her sixth child, declined. She and Oswald disembarked at Cape Town intending to travel overland to Kuruman and, when fit, rejoin Livingstone on the Zambezi. A tumultuous reception, one altogether different from the cool welcome he had received some 17 years previously, awaited Livingstone at the Cape. He was given a grand dinner and presented with a 'testimonial box' containing 800 guineas.

The plan was to move quickly through the lower, unhealthy stretches of the Zambezi and then establish a depot to serve as a centre for both agricultural experiments and religious instruction. The Zambezi would then be explored, first as far as Tette where the heavy loads would be landed, then on to the Kebrabasa Rapids 50 miles (80 km) further upstream.

Livingstone's party set out from Kongona, at the mouth of the Zambezi, in October 1858. Several journeys were needed by the *Ma-Robert* to transport the supplies to Shupanga, 75 miles (120 km) upstream. The party then pressed on another 50 miles (80 km) to Sena, a depressing and dilapidated village where, according to Livingstone 'one is sure to take fever on the second day – that is, if by chance one has missed it on the first day.'

The expedition set out with great promise, but problems soon arose. Despite Livingstone's enormous ability to command the allegiance of Africans, he was unable to weld his varied collection of experts into a cohesive team. They, in turn, were unprepared for the demanding climate, the sheer monotony of the trek and the debilitating fevers. In addition, the local Portuguese governors were markedly unimpressed by the letters addressed to them. They considered the expedition an intrusion and were concerned, not without good cause, that one of Livingstone's objects was to sabotage their lucrative slave-trading activities.

The naval commander recruited as second-in-command proved particularly recalcitrant. Livingstone, with delightful Victorian phraseology, described him as ' an unmitigated muff'. There were faults on both sides but the acrimony resulted in the commander's resignation. Livingstone himself then took command of the boat, though he confessed that he often got his starboard muddled with his port – which in crocodile-infested rivers is never a good thing. There was also increasing resentment among the crew at Livingstone's inability to recognize the indolence of his brother. A biographer writing nearly 50 years ago questioned whether it was misguided loyalty or sentimental attachment which prevented Livingstone realizing that his brother 'really was, the weakest link'.

As the *Ma-Robert* chugged on, the river shoals worsened and the vessel constantly grounded, but by early November the party reached Tette. Livingstone was anxious not to delay and set out for the Kebrabasa Rapids a couple of days later. The early rains had started and the rapids, he found, were 'fearful when in flood', and likely to rise 80 feet (24 m) when the rains were at their height. In the dry season, the vicious rocks prevented passage but come the rains, Livingstone thought, the river might be navigable though not by the *Ma-Robert* which was at best grossly under-powered and painfully slow, consuming enormous quantities of fuel. It took over an hour to build up enough steam to move her at all. She snorted and wheezed so much that the crew nicknamed her the *Asthmatic*. Livingstone's answer was to demand a new boat from the government. Fearing that nothing would be forthcoming, he authorized a friend to purchase one on his behalf – at a cost of £6,000, the greater part of the remaining profits from his book. In the event, the government did in fact supply one, the *Pioneer*. Livingstone's purchase was christened the *Lady Nyassa* though it was to be some while before the boats could be delivered. In the mean time, the expedition struggled on with the *Ma-Robert*.

Malaria had again become a major problem. In his journal, Livingstone described in detail his prescription for anti-malarial pills. He also commented that, for the first time, he was beginning to find them ineffective – perhaps an early indication of how mosquitoes can build up resistance to particular drugs.

After a temporary return to Tette, Livingstone set out again for the rapids. On reaching the furthest point possible with the *Ma-Robert*, he selected a few from the crew and set off on foot to investigate reports of other rapids further upstream. It meant gruelling, tortuous climbs up blistering hot rocks to 1,500 feet (450 m), then 1,000 foot (300 m) descents with no shade from the unrelenting sun – then up again. It was difficult to travel more than a mile in each hour.

Livingstone's private journal gives glimpses of his depression at this time, suggesting that he was beginning to realize that failure was unavoidable. He had staked everything on finding a route to the interior, but it was becoming increasingly clear that no such route existed.

Evidence of the slave trade was never far away. Livingstone describes in graphic detail the departure by boat from Tette of 20 men and 40 women, all in chains, to be sold further downstream. Such examples were common occurrences. He also illustrated the 'slave-stick' used when slaves were first captured. This consisted of a forked pole, the neck of the slave being tied into the fork. The slave was led by this stick, tied to other sticks, until he – or she – was sufficiently 'tame' to be put in chains.

UP THE SHIRÉ

The second stage of the operation was to explore the previously uncharted **River Shiré** which runs northwards from the Zambezi to the southern tip of Lake Nyasa. The first attempt was halted after a few days by rapids which Livingstone named the Murchison Cataracts. The area was well populated and suspicious crowds armed with bows and poisoned arrows followed them. Livingstone placated them by explaining that he and his party were English, not Portuguese, and were not out to capture slaves. He notes, in his journal, that cleanliness was not one of their virtues and that a follower who became too

KEYWORD

River Shiré (16.30S, 35.0E) is the most important river in Malawi. Two hundred and fifty miles (400 km) long, it is the only outlet for Lake Nyasa and drops 1,260 feet (385 m) to the Zambezi through a series of cataracts and gorges. Today, an important hydro-electric power centre is located there.

persistent ran away when Livingstone threatened to wash him. He also found the lip and nose ornamentation of the ladies highly disagreeable.

On the second Shiré journey a detour was made to the east, resulting in the discovery of Lake Shirwa (now called Lake Chilwa) which Livingstone described in a letter to his daughter as 'a magnificent inland lake surrounded by 6000 foot high mountains'. A third voyage along the Shiré was made a few months later when **Lake Nyasa** itself was discovered.

The closing months of 1859 saw Livingstone's health beginning to break down with constant bleeding from his bowels, a condition which was to remain with him until his death. However, he was cheered by news of the birth of a daughter, almost a year previously, back at Kuruman. News did not travel fast in those days.

The *Ma-Robert* continued to give problems and 1860 began with it needing substantial repairs. The rest of the year was taken up with further exploration of the Zambezi. Livingstone trudged through to Victoria Falls again and found they were much larger than his original estimates. He also received sad news of the deaths from fever of some earlier missionaries who had set up stations in the area; there was little left of their work. The year ended with the disaster-prone *Ma-Robert* becoming stranded on a sandbank and defying all attempts to re-float her. She had to be abandoned.

KEYWORD

Lake Nyasa (12.30S, 34.30E, also called Lake Malawi) is 363 miles (584 km) long (greater than the length of England) the width varying from 10 to 50 miles (16–80 km). At its northern end, it is 2,310 feet (704 m) deep. It is the most southern and third largest of the Rift Valley lakes. Fed by 14 rivers, the Shiré is its only outlet. The Portu-guese Caspar Boccaro first reported its existence in the sixteenth century. Livingstone was first to reach the southern end in 1859. The *Mwera* wind blows, sometimes at gale force, May–August, causing rough water. Since the length of the lake is parallel to the coast, it gives access to a wide span of the Interior. Today, commercial fisheries exist at the lake's southern end. Passenger and cargo vessels operate on the lake carrying cotton, rubber, rice, tung oil and groundnuts. (Nyasa used to be spelt with a double 's'. The modern spelling with a single 's' is used in this text except for the name of Livingstone's boat.)

Livingstone continued to be appalled at the indifference of the Portuguese towards the Africans whom they claimed to rule and by the continual wars between the African tribes. These bloody struggles could desolate whole areas of the country. From time to time, a strong leader would emerge who would unify the tribes in the area but, on his death, war would again break out between rivals.

Livingstone was considerably impressed with the area's potential for development and settlement. With broad cool plateaux rising to 3,000 feet (900 m), the Shiré valley struck him as highly suitable for colonization. He felt that, after all, his vision of the past ten years might be realized. The huge areas of fertile land, he considered, could grow sufficient produce to meet all the needs of Europe – thus doing away with reliance on slave-grown products from the Americas. He was certain that the local people, whom he regarded as extremely industrious, could and would grow much, much more if only they could sell it. The idea of Christian colonization fascinated Livingstone. Fresh European blood, he suggested, should be poured into Africa, especially that of 'the honest poor … particularly the healthy blooming daughters of England' whom he considered to be 'the most beautiful women of the world'. And, with an implied criticism of the colonization of Australia, he added in his private journal that the immigrants should be chosen, *not* from 'the female emigrants from workhouses (which) send forth the ugliest huzzies in creation to be the mothers of the Empire…as if the worst as well as the better qualities of mankind do not run in the blood'.

It is ironic that Stanley, who was to become one of his closest friends and who, some years later, saved Livingstone's life when he was hopelessly destitute in the bush, was an *emigré* from a workhouse.

✳ ✳ ✳ SUMMARY ✳ ✳ ✳

- Livingstone received a great reception on returning to England and was awarded many honours.

- His book *Missionary Travels and Researches in South Africa* became an instant best-seller.

- He accepted a government offer to explore the Zambezi and, with his family, returned to Africa.

- Health problems forced Mrs Livingstone to disembark at Cape Town and travel to Kuruman where she later gave birth to a daughter.

- Livingstone first explored the Zambezi as far as the Kebrabasa Rapids but found the *Ma-Robert* unequal to the task. He requested a replacement from the government. He also ordered one privately.

- He then made three explorations of the Shiré, discovering Lake Shirwa and entering Lake Nyasa from the south.

Change of fortunes, 1861–63

7

NEW HOPES, MORE PROBLEMS

The year 1861 began well with the arrival of the *Pioneer*, the British government's replacement for the *Ma-Robert*. First impressions were that she would be a big improvement on the old boat. A number of fledgling missionaries led by Bishop Mackensie also arrived intending to establish a mission station on the Shiré River. Although only 36, Mackensie, an outstanding scholar, had been appointed as the first Missionary Bishop of England

Livingstone's brief was to explore the **Rovuma River** and to check whether it provided a route through to Lake Nyasa. He was then to take the bishop to his station on the Shiré. Problems soon arose particularly from the deeper draught of the new boat. By the time the bishop had arrived, the water level in the Rovuma River had already fallen and the *Pioneer* constantly grounded. This forced Livingstone to postpone the expedition until after he had transported the bishop's party to their new home. The slave trade was being pursued ever more vigorously and the Portuguese had become very antagonistic towards Livingstone. The promises which he had been given by the Portuguese government before leaving England proved valueless. Slave-hunting chiefs were roaming the region destroying the crops and villages of neighbouring tribes, seizing men, women and children to be sold as slaves – and killing many more in the process. Their indifference to the sufferings of their own kind was unbelievable. 'Slaves cost nothing' Hamed bin Mohammed, a notorious Arab slave-trader said a few years later to H. M. Stanley, 'they only have to be gathered'. Livingstone found a 100-mile (160 km) stretch of country completely de-populated where, just two years previously, there had been villages every few miles. Because local people often thought Livingstone himself was a slaver, they gave him little co-operation. In fact, he experienced his first-ever violent confrontation when he and the bishop were obliged to resort to firearms to repel attackers. The extent of the slave trade was summarized in a report by **Colonel Rigby**, British Consul in Zanzibar. He estimated that, every year, 19,000 slaves from the Lake Nyasa region alone passed through the Zanzibar Customs House. That did not include those going through other east-coast ports. Four times that number were killed during raids or died later, either from wounds or from starvation after their crops had been burnt.

KEYWORD

Colonel (later Major General) C. P. Rigby, HM Consul at Zanzibar in Livingstone's time did more to suppress the slave trade than any other man of his generation. He was also entrusted with the task of transporting Livingstone's body from Southampton to Westminster Abbey. An excellent biography of him was written by his daughter (Mrs C. E. B. Russell) who later worked with Dr Schweitzer.

THE SHIRÉ EXPEDITION

After installing the bishop, Livingstone planned to sail further up the Shiré, enter Lake Nyasa and then investigate whether access to the Rovuma from the lake's east bank existed. After the *Pioneer* had again grounded in the Shiré, Livingstone with his brother and another colleague carried on upstream in a four-oared boat which was carried by porters past the Murchison Cataracts. He succeeded in reaching the lake, but shortage of stores forced him to abandon the attempt to reach the Rovuma – which was doomed to failure anyway because, unbeknown at the time, the Rovuma did not reach the lake. Its source lay elsewhere.

A plan to return to the mouth of the Zambezi to pick up stores from a warship was delayed because the *Pioneer* was stuck for five weeks on sandbanks and the rendezvous date was missed. During the delay, the ship's carpenter died from fever. It was the first of several deaths which Livingstone had to cope with in the weeks which followed.

January 1862 saw the arrival on the Zambezi of HMS *Gorgon* carrying Mrs Livingstone, Miss Mackensie (the sister of the bishop) and Mrs Burrup, wife of the Reverend Burrup, one of the bishop's colleagues. The *Gorgon* had in tow a boat carrying the dismantled *Lady Nyassa*, the boat Livingstone had purchased. The parts were quickly transferred to the *Pioneer*, the plan being to assemble the new boat at Shupanga. Overloaded and constantly grounding, the *Pioneer* chugged its way up the Zambezi.

TRAGEDY STRIKES

Just 11 months after their arrival on the Zambezi, both Bishop Mackensie and the Reverend Burrup died in an accident. They had been on their way to pick up their newly arrived relatives when their canoe overturned. Exhausted, both managed to scramble ashore but they succumbed to fever, possibly pneumonia. Livingstone had to break the sad news to the two ladies who were looking forward to a happy reunion. The deaths meant further delays as the *Pioneer* then had to return to the mouth of the Zambezi for the two bereaved ladies to rejoin the *Gorgon* for passage home.

The *Pioneer* eventually reached Shupanga and work on assembling the *Lady Nyassa* began. But a further sad event awaited Livingstone. On 21 April 1862, Mrs Livingstone became very ill, probably with malaria. As the days passed, her condition worsened. Within the week, she became delirious and sank into a deep coma. Although Livingstone realized death was near, her passing on 27 April completely shattered him. He wept like a child and, in his private journal, confessed that it was the first time in his life that he wished to die.

Mrs Livingstone was buried beside a large baobab tree, some 60 feet (18 m) in circumference, on the banks of the Zambezi.

Had Livingstone been right to set such great priority on exploration even to the detriment of the welfare of his wife and children? He dragged the family around the most inhospitable parts of Africa with Mary giving birth under the most primitive conditions. She suffered penury in

England whilst he spent major sums on other purposes. By today's standards, most would say emphatically 'No'. But care must be taken in judging yesterday's behaviour by today's standards. Livingstone was a product of his age, as indeed we all are. He lived in times when wives had few rights, not even that of retaining ownership of their own pre-nuptial property. It was the accepted norm that a wife should serve her husband's wishes, no matter what that might entail. There is no doubt he loved his wife deeply – and she him. But were the demands he made upon his family excessive even by nineteenth-century standards? Judging from the criticism he received from so many quarters, particularly from Dr Moffat who knew so well the conditions, one can be excused for answering 'Yes'.

Should he have married in the first place? Bearing in mind the life he was to live, it might well have been better if he had not – but it must be remembered that, at the time of his marriage, he was expecting to live a settled life at a mission station at Mabotsa where Mary was to undertake the essential task of establishing a primary school. Only subsequently did he feel himself called to exploration. Whether he should then have become an explorer – and, more cogently, whether he should have *continued* as an explorer once he realized the demands it would make on his family – is a more difficult question to answer. But would a reasonable and compassionate man, one willing to listen to others and conscious of the needs of his family, have achieved what Livingstone did? And would the world have been a poorer place if he had not?

MORE ATTEMPTS TO REACH LAKE NYASA

It was not long before Livingstone braced himself to return to work and by June 1862, the *Lady Nyassa* had been assembled. Local helpers were amazed when the iron hull floated. The boat would have been excellent for work on Lake Nyasa but, because the rains were now over, she was unable to navigate the rapids. Instead, Livingstone decided to go back to the Rovuma still hoping to find a route through to Lake Nyasa. Unfortunately, the idea had to be abandoned when cataracts 150 miles (240 km) upstream halted the expedition and information was received that the source of the Rovuma was not Lake Nyasa but in the mountains to the east of the lake.

Early in 1863 Livingstone set sail in the *Pioneer* with the *Lady Nyassa* in tow for another attempt to reach Lake Nyasa via the Zambezi and the Shiré. He grew increasingly appalled at the ongoing growth of the slave trade. Although prohibited on the ocean, it was still legal on land. Anyone interfering with the captives of slave-traders was guilty of robbery under Portuguese law. The killings continued unabated. Livingstone describes how a steady stream of corpses floated by as his boat steamed northwards and how, every morning, bodies had to be cleared from the ship's paddles. At one point Livingstone took a walk through what 18 months previously had been a well-populated valley. He found it deserted with human skeletons lying in grotesque heaps in every direction. He concluded that unless the slave trade – that 'monster iniquity which has brooded over Africa for so long' – could be ended, there was little hope for the future.

THE EXPEDITION RECALLED

Livingstone's reverse of fortunes did not end with the series of deaths, nor with the failure of the Shiré and Rovuma missions or with his terrible experiences of the slave trade. In July 1863, the British government recalled his party on the grounds that, through no fault of Livingstone, the objectives of the expedition had not been achieved and the cost was proving far too much. There was also a political aspect in that Livingstone's methods were 'not considered consistent with the rights of the Portuguese government'. Livingstone took the disappointment stoically, consoling himself with the thought that on the Portuguese, and not on himself, 'lay the guilt of arresting a work that would have conferred untold blessing on Africa'. In his journal, he quoted Robert Burns's prophetic statement – one which is even more relevant to the world today than it was when written – that 'man's inhumanity to man makes countless thousands mourn'.

The call of Africa remained in Livingstone's blood. He decided to struggle on to Lake Nyasa on foot without government support. But it was not easy. His small party got lost in the jungle, were unable to obtain any guides and had several narrow escapes when mistaken for Portuguese slave-traders. He managed to reach the Loangwa, a river which flows into the lake midway up its western shoreline and, throughout September, explored some of its upper reaches. But Livingstone had then to call a halt. Several of the party had been taken ill; one had died. Finally, the British government insisted the *Pioneer*, which was their property, should be returned. This meant returning to the boat and sailing her back to the mouth of the Zambezi once the river was in full flood. This left him no time to explore further.

THE FINAL BLOW

Livingstone reached the *Pioneer* in November 1863 but the rains were late and he had to wait two months for the river to rise sufficiently. During that time, Livingstone's great hope of a few years before received its final blow. It came in a letter from Bishop Tozer who had succeeded Mackensie at the Shiré Mission, stating that he intended to close the centre as the Portuguese were making life impossible. Livingstone urged Tozer to reconsider but he was adamant. Livingstone was particularly worried about the welfare of those who sheltered there – a few elderly people, some young boys and several rescued slaves. Tozer would not accept responsibility for them, so the ever-philanthropic Livingstone arranged for their transport to safety at the Cape at his own expense. He directed a friend who was managing the transfer that, should any Portuguese interfere with them on the journey, they should be 'pitched overboard'.

One can understand his feelings, even though he was a missionary.

Although Livingstone returned home with his life's work in apparent ruins, his absence from Africa was to be for only a few months. He would return to look, once again, for a new route into the Interior.

* * * SUMMARY * * *

- The arrival of two new boats promised much, but Livingstone's hopes were progressively and tragically shattered.

- The *Pioneer* had too deep a draught for river work.

- The passing of the rainy season prevented the *Lady Nyassa* reaching the lake.

- Mrs Livingstone, Bishop Mackensie, the Reverend Burrup, and others, died.

- Attempts to find a route from the Rovuma to Lake Nyasa, and from Lake Nyasa to the Rovuma, both failed.

- The Shiré mission station was closed by Mackensie's successor.

- The expedition was recalled.

- 1863 ended with many of Livingstone's hopes and ambitions shattered.

8 Second home leave, 1864-67

HEADING FOR ENGLAND

The trip back to England was eventful. Livingstone was escorted from the mouth of the Zambezi to Mozambique by two naval boats – one towing the *Lady Nyassa* with Livingstone on board and one towing the *Pioneer*. A day out of port, the ships met a fierce storm which would have sunk many a lesser ship, but the *Lady Nyassa* rode it well, increasing Livingstone's regret that no opportunity had existed to sail the boat on Lake Nyasa.

The *Pioneer* was duly handed over to the Royal Navy. The Portuguese had wanted to buy the *Lady Nyassa* for slaving purposes, but understandably Livingstone said he would rather send the boat to the bottom of the Indian Ocean than allow that. Instead, he resolved to sail it himself from Mozambique, with himself as skipper, first to Zanzibar and then to Bombay. He recruited as crew a stoker, a carpenter, an experienced sailor and nine Zambezians, one of whom was Chuma – the one who was to be with him at his death. It was to be a 2,500-mile (4,000 km) voyage over an ocean Livingstone had never crossed. He estimated the journey would take 18 days; in fact it took 45 as the ship was becalmed for three weeks. Supplies ran desperately short. But Bombay was eventually reached. After visiting several mission schools, Livingstone arranged for the *Lady Nyassa* to be laid up pending sale and then left for England.

HOME LEAVE

Livingstone reached England in July 1865. He was immediately caught up in a whirl of engagements. On his first evening, he visited Sir Roderick Murchison, President of the Royal Geographical Society, and was then whisked off to a reception given by Lord Palmerston, the Prime Minister. The following day he was at the Foreign Office after which he attended the Duchess of Wellington's reception. He described the ladies there as 'wonderfully beautiful'. The day after he met Lord Russell, whose manner he considered 'cold'. He also received an invitation to dinner from the Lord Mayor in order to meet government ministers. Two days later he was again dining with the Prime Minister, having met Gladstone earlier in the day. The sumptuous dinners which suddenly became his daily fare must have been difficult to digest after his meagre diet in Africa. After a rest in Scotland, he made several major speeches. The Portuguese government took great exception to one given to the British Association at Bath describing the Portuguese involvement in the slave trade. This was to have unfortunate repercussions for him on his later return to Africa.

But it was not all bright lights and high living. The day he dined with the Lord Mayor he received the sad news of his son Robert's death. Robert had joined the Federal Army in America under an assumed name in order to fight in the Civil War. The lad was only 19 when he died of wounds in a prisoner-of-war camp. He is buried at the Gettysburgh National Cemetery, the site of Lincoln's famous address.

Livingstone also had health problems. He seriously considered having surgery for the haemorrhoids which had troubled him for so long. After some thought, he decided against it, partly because of conflicting medical advice and partly because he did not wish to publicize his condition. This was probably a great mistake, as it was the constant internal bleeding caused by his complaint, and the breakdown of the colon wall, that was the prime cause of his death. But it is easy to be wise with hindsight. Haemorrhoidectomy is still, today, one of the more painful operations and, in Livingstone's time, anaesthetics and analgesics were not commonly available. Livingstone must have seen many cases where the operation had been unsuccessful. Instead, he accepted an invitation to shut himself away in Newstead Abbey and write a book about his travels under the title *The Zambezi and its Tributaries*. It took him eight months to complete.

Livingstone intended to use the royalties to finance further explorations of the Rovuma River as he wished to establish a settlement far away, as he thought, from the Portuguese who had ruined so much of his previous work. By coincidence, early in January of 1866 and shortly before he completed the book, Livingstone was invited by Sir Roderick Murchison and the Royal Geographical Society to undertake just such an adventure. Its primary purpose would be to investigate whether the river formed a route to the west coast. Also, whether it was possible to reach the southern shores of Lake Tanganyika – the large lake north of Lake Nyasa – and of locating the source of the Nile. This was a topic of burning interest to the geographers of the day as well to Livingstone. He hoped that the Nile, if it extended that far, could provide a route to Central Africa from the Mediterranean. The vital question was where did the watershed in Africa lie? No one knew and anyone solving that problem would have received worldwide recognition.

Livingstone gladly agreed to the proposition, although he realized that, in accepting the challenge, critics would argue that he had put aside his missionary commitment for the sake of exploration and the fame which went with it. His habit of preferring to be addressed as David Livingstone Esq rather than as the Reverend Dr Livingstone, together with his customary dress of plaid trousers, blue coat with gilt buttons, red shirt and a peaked cap with gold band, did little to impress the missionary diehards. His own view was that, as an explorer intent on opening up a heathen continent to Christianity – and in doing so undermining the slave trade – he was likely to have far more influence for good than working simply as a missionary. He did, however, make it clear that he would only accept the commission provided he went primarily as a missionary and undertook the geographic research only as a secondary commitment.

Before his departure, the Foreign Office offered Livingstone the position of British Consul in East Africa, a post carrying no salary or pension rights. Livingstone thought it altogether a shabby deal but accepted it in order to add a degree of status to his position.

THE RETURN JOURNEY TO AFRICA

Livingstone returned to Africa via Paris where he settled his daughter in school. He then travelled down to Marseilles and from there to Bombay which he reached in September 1865. On the trip, he saw the final part of the Suez Canal being constructed, the opening of which was later covered by the reporter H. M. Stanley who subsequently 'found' him on the banks of Lake Tanganyika.

In India, Livingstone sold the *Lady Nyassa* for less than half its original cost. He deposited the money in a local bank which later failed – and he lost all the money. From Bombay, he sailed to Zanzibar in the *Thule* which he described as 'the most incorrigible roller I have ever known'. He had to kick his heels in Zanzibar for two months whilst awaiting the arrival of HMS *Penguin* which was to take him to the mouth of the Rovuma. During that time, he had to suffer the existence of the slave markets and the daily sight of slave boats arriving and departing. He used the time to recruit 35 African retainers to sail with him. He also took six camels, three buffaloes, two mules and four donkeys in an accompanying **dhow**. He wished to check whether the animals would be resistant to tsetse flies, regarded as much the scourge of animals as mosquitoes were of man.

KEYWORD

Dhows are Arab vessels with high-windowed, decorated sterns and huge lateen-rigged triangular sails. Most now have auxiliary diesel engines. Following the monsoon winds, dhows have sailed between Arabia, Persia and Africa for centuries, and continue to do so today. Tourists relaxing on the sun-bleached East African beaches still wonder at the sight of their huge sails gliding silently with poetic grace along the coastline beyond the coral reef.

THE SLAVE PROBLEM AGAIN

Livingstone disembarked at the mouth of the Rovuma in the spring of 1866. He soon ran into difficulties. Some men had to be discharged immediately as they had treated the animals so badly. Then, as he moved upcountry towards Lake Nyasa, slave parties became increasingly common. Evidence of the horrors of the trade were there for all to witness. Bones, skulls and distorted skeletons were everywhere. Women, exhausted by the journey, had been tied to trees and left to die a miserable death in the heat. Every path was littered with the corpses of Africans who had been shot or stabbed. Other bodies – some still in slave-sticks – lay dying from their wounds. Most were captives who had been unable to keep up with the slave-party. It was the custom of both the Arabs and the Portuguese to kill such people so as to deny their usefulness to others.

Livingstone planned to follow the Rovuma to its upper reaches, then cut across to Lake Nyasa. From there, he aimed to strike north to Lake Tanganyika. It took him three months to cut his way through the bush to Lake Nyasa. He arrived there to find that, because of his record as an outspoken anti-slaver, the Portuguese were unwilling to sell or hire him a boat and he had to tramp round the shore line. Livingstone's problems were compounded by a group of retainers who deserted him and returned to Zanzibar saying he had been murdered. They told the story primarily so that they could claim their pay. The account was widely believed both in Africa and back in England, though there were some doubters. So strong were the doubts at the Royal Geographical Society that, some months later, an expedition was sent out to check the report. It sailed up the Rovuma in a boat appropriately named the *Search*. After an eight-month investigation, clear evidence was found that Livingstone had been seen alive long *after* the deserters had left him, meaning that their accounts of his death had been untrue.

Livingstone himself, at this time, was pressing on towards Lake Tanganyika. Most of his animals, including the goats, had died which meant he was without milk as well as being desperately short of food. Hunger was becoming a serious problem and he was forced to survive on a restricted diet of African maize – a far cry, as he pointed out in a letter to his son Thomas, from the roast beef of old England. He must have experienced acute nostalgia for the excellent banquets he had enjoyed during his home visits.

Livingstone now suffered the greatest calamity of the trip, one which he compared with a sentence of death. His medicine chest was stolen. Although normally carried by a very responsible member of his party, it had been entrusted to a porter who had been hired for the day. He decamped with it and neither he nor the medicines were ever seen again. For four long years – until, in fact, his meeting with Stanley – Livingstone was without any medicines with which to combat his recurrent fever and other ailments. He was, by this time, suffering from lung and foot infections as well as from the ongoing troubles with his bowels.

The loss of that medicine chest was probably the beginning of the end for Livingstone.

* * *SUMMARY* * *

- In February 1864, Livingstone met two naval ships at the mouth of the Zambezi which towed his own two boats to Mozambique.

- After handing the *Pioneer* over to the Navy, he sailed the *Lady Nyassa* first to Zanzibar, then to Bombay where the boat was laid up pending sale.

- Livingstone arrived back in England in July 1864.

- The Portuguese took great exception to a speech he gave to the British Association.

- Livingstone wrote a book describing his travels along the Zambezi. He planned to use the royalties to finance further exploration of the Rovuma. Before its completion, the Royal Geographical Society invited him to undertake just such an expedition.

- In Bombay on his return trip to Africa, Livingstone sold the *Lady Nyassa*, then sailed for Zanzibar.

- HMS *Penguin* transported Livingstone's party to the mouth of the Rovuma where he had to discharge some of his servants. As he moved upcountry, Livingstone was appalled by the horrific evidence of the slave trade.

- Livingstone reached Lake Nyasa in August 1866. A group of his men deserted and spread a widely believed rumour – later proved false – that he had been murdered.

- Livingstone's medicine chest was stolen in early 1867. This was a serious blow.

9 Westward from Lake Tanganyika, 1867–71

DISCOVERY OF LAKES MOERO AND BANGWEOLO

During early 1867 Livingstone and the surviving members of his party struggled on and were rewarded, in April, by the sight of the southern tip of **Lake Tanganyika** – then known as Lake Liemba – originally discovered by John Speke and Richard Burton in 1858. Livingstone avoided visiting the lake itself because of reports of killings taking place there. His pleasure at finding the lake was tempered by a severe bout of fever which, without medicines, he was unable to treat. When recovered, he decided to forge on and in November 1867 discovered Lake Moero (sometimes spelt Mueru or Mweru), a smaller lake lying to the west of Lake Tanganyika. Reports of a much larger lake to the south made him decide to search for it and this resulted in the discovery, in July 1868, of the massive Lake Bemba, now known as **Lake Bangweolo**, and its associated swamp. He thought, mistakenly, that the lake was the source of three major rivers – the Lualaba, the Congo and the Nile. It was left for others to prove that the Lualaba was in fact the Congo, and that there was no link with the Nile.

After surveying the lake, Livingstone set out for Ujiji, a town near Kigoma on the north-east shores of Lake Tanganyika, where he hoped food, medical supplies and letters would be waiting since it was over two years since he had received

KEYWORDS

Lake Tanganyika (6.40S, 30.0E) is the second largest lake in Africa, the world's second deepest (1,436 m) and longest fresh-water lake (470 miles or 756 km). It contains one-sixth of the world's reserves of fresh water which is mainly brackish but hippo-potamuses (which kill more people in Africa than any other animal), crocodiles and bird life abound.

Lake Bangweolo (11.20S, 30.15E) and its associated swamp covers an area the size of Wales. The swamp dries up during the dry season. The local barbel fish (or 'lung-fish') which evolved over 300 million years ago survive in mud until the rains return, making use of their primitive lung structure. Their gills also serve as makeshift limbs enabling them to search for ponds.

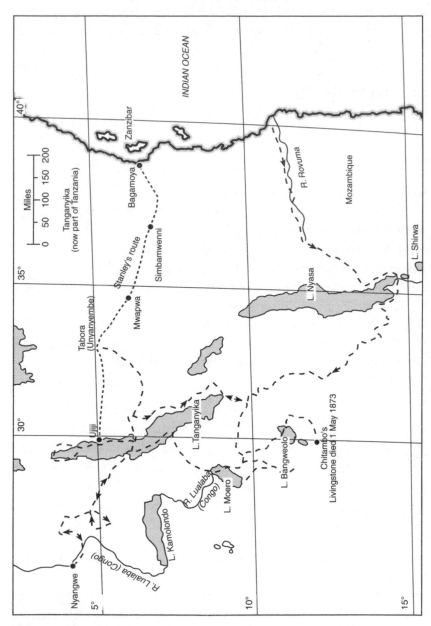

Livingstone's last journeys, 1867–72, and the route taken by Stanley, 1871–2

any home news. It was not long before he again fell seriously ill with a very high fever. Unable to stop coughing, hardly able to move and with no medicines available, he still wanted to strive on. In delirium, he lost track of time and was forced to accept help from some Arab slave-traders who were making their way to Ujiji. They carried him in a makeshift litter over the rough ground, his face but poorly protected from the sun. On reaching the southern shore of Lake Tanganyika, Livingstone was transferred to a canoe and eventually reached Ujiji in March – only to find that tribal wars had prevented any supplies or mail arriving.

SEARCH FOR THE LUALABA

Livingstone arrived at Ujiji in March 1869 but did not spend any longer recuperating there than necessary. The slave-traders in the district were 'scum and riff-raff' even by slave-trading standards – the ones he had met previously were gentlemen by comparison. During his rest, he wrote over 40 long letters, but none was ever received. In June 1869, Livingstone decided to explore the country north-west of Lake Tanganyika, hoping to track down the River Lualaba. He still believed that this river could, in fact, be the Nile and that his observations would settle the whole question of the watershed pattern in Africa.

Livingstone now entered notorious cannibal territory. The going became very rough. In September 1869, he reached a town called Bambarre and, after a short rest, carried on westwards to the Luamo River, a tributary of the Lualaba. Believing he was just another slave-trader, the local people were very uncooperative and refused him canoes. Unable to go any further, he returned to Bambarre where the rains forced him to remain until the end of June 1870 when he set out again. The weather, fallen trees and flooded rivers made travel extremely difficult. The sores on his feet, instead of healing, became so infected that he had to abandon the expedition and limp back to Bambarre. He had to rest in a hut for more than two months.

The privations over the years had taken their toll on Livingstone's physique. Eating was difficult with his few remaining teeth, his eyes were sunken and his illnesses had left him little more than a living skeleton. He was still bitterly disappointed at the failure of the Shiré mission and he began to accept that he seemed to have done no more than open up Africa for the slavers. He still sorely missed his wife; it had been some years since he had last heard from home – and since people at home had heard from him. In fact, there was considerable speculation whether he was still alive. He had an intense longing to retire from Africa but he was not prepared to leave unfinished the tasks that he had set out to do.

By the end of 1871 he was feeling better and in February 1872 set off again. By March, he had reached Nyangwe on the banks of the Lualaba River. But he was to face a further disappointment – the river flowed to the south and could not be the source of the Nile. Further, local resentment again meant that he was unable to obtain canoes for more detailed explorations – which was as well as he later learned there were dangerous rapids with which the canoes could not have coped. Outbreaks of violent tribal disturbances and massacres in the area added to his troubles. To cap it all, the pain from his haemorrhoids had become excruciating and his intestinal canal began to give way causing almost continual severe bleeding.

RETURN TO UJIJI

He decided to return to Ujiji. Despite his declining physical condition, he hoped to recruit new men for yet another attempt to explore the Lualaba. The journey back to Ujiji was a frightening experience. Local tribesmen were convinced he was a slave-trader and set many ambushes from which he narrowly escaped with his life. In one day alone, he had three narrow brushes with death: a spear grazed his neck, another missed him by a few inches and a tree, felled by fire, crashed within a yard of him. In addition, more of his supplies were lost and he was becoming increasingly ill. On 23 October1871, he staggered into Ujiji.

Five days later, a saviour appeared. It was Henry Morton Stanley, carrying ample stores and medicines.

'DR LIVINGSTONE, I PRESUME?'

But for that simple salutation on the banks of Lake Tanganyika in the autumn of 1871 it is possible that few of us today would ever have heard of Stanley. It alone resulted in their names becoming inextricably linked. A most unlikely friendship developed between two very different men.

The sheer urbanity of the greeting made it a standing joke – so much so that even today it still figures high in light-hearted banter. It was to haunt Stanley for the rest his life. Often he wished that he had never said it. As time went by, the phrase became so legendary that some began to doubt whether it had ever actually been said. When asked long after he had retired whether the story was true, Stanley simply replied, 'Well, what else *could* I have said?'

Like Livingstone, Stanley had a poverty-constrained background. Unlike Livingstone, it was a sad, almost bizarre one – a most unlikely start for a person who ultimately achieved the fame and fortune that Stanley did. Born at Denbigh, Wales, on 28 January 1841, 27 years Livingstone's junior, he was the illegitimate son of Elizabeth Parry, a servant in a London household and of John Rowlands, a farmer who was reputedly killed in a pub brawl. His mother has often been criticized for abandoning him soon after birth, but it is difficult to understand these days the slur which illegitimacy used to cast upon both child and mother. She must have found herself in an impossible position with little option but to leave her son to be brought up by his grandfather whilst she returned to 'service' in London.

The lad was christened John Rowlands after his father. He did not adopt the name 'Stanley' until late in his teens. His grandfather looked after him until his death five years later. For a few months thereafter, Stanley was supported (resentfully) by two uncles. At age six, they placed him in a workhouse. The Poor Law Act of 1601 required 'the parish' to maintain all paupers, orphans, foundlings, insane and destitute – which meant accommodating them in the local workhouse. Readers of *Oliver Twist* will know just what sort of conditions existed in such establishments.

They were dens of depravity and vice with sexual and physical abuse a daily occurrence. The young Stanley soon learnt that any sign of weakness on his part would merit a beating, either by his fellow inmates or by the workhouse master whose joy was to give some hapless youngster a sound flogging.

Working hours lasted from early morning till late at night. The only education Stanley received – never more than two hours a day and usually less – was learning by rote the catechism and long passages of scripture. Stanley was conscious all his life of the stigma associated with illegitimacy and with having grown up in a workhouse – the experience left an indelible mark on his personality. Biographers often describe him as being lonely, silent, aloof, unfriendly and devoid of any sense of humour – not surprising, given his background.

Workhouse life left Stanley with a burning desire to succeed whatever the odds. Surprisingly, it also left him with a firm belief in a Christianity backed by a literal interpretation of the Bible. He also learnt that the best way to solve problems was with his fists – a procedure he often used years later in the African bush to quell potential rebellions among his men.

When 15, Stanley had a violent altercation with the workhouse master which left the fellow unconscious on the floor. Stanley, perhaps wisely, ran away and for a couple of years lived with an aunt who gave him a home but showed him no more love than had his uncles. When aged 17, another aunt took him to Liverpool where he worked as an errand boy often visiting the docks. The boats – and all the activity around them – fascinated him. The result was that, just before Christmas 1851, he joined a ship bound for New Orleans as a cabin boy – though, once aboard, he was treated as an unpaid deckhand. He 'jumped ship' in New Orleans and, penniless, began to search for work. Eventually, a sympathetic merchant gave him a job as a storekeeper. Stanley was so grateful he adopted the merchant's name – Henry Stanley. 'Morton' was Stanley's own addition. Shortly afterwards, the merchant went to visit a sick brother. The sick brother recovered but the merchant died, though Stanley was unaware of this until some years later.

With the outbreak of the American Civil War, Stanley was cajoled into joining the Confederate (i.e. Southern) army. Captured in battle, he avoided becoming a prisoner of war by agreeing to fight for the Unionist (Northern) side. Appalled at the death, destruction and human suffering he saw on the battlefield, he lost his Christian faith – and did not regain it until he found solace in the massive solitude of the African bush.

After the war, he became a merchant seaman, then joined the US Navy. His reports of the battles he saw made him realize he had a talent for writing. As a consequence, he deserted and went to New York, working as a journalist for a number of papers. He then obtained a temporary job covering a war in Abyssinia (now Ethiopia) with the *New York Herald* – a widely read 'popular' newspaper which, at that time, tended to let the factual take second-place to the sensational. Most intellectuals derided the paper – Livingstone himself described it as 'that despicable newspaper'. Stanley stole a march on other reporters by getting his war reports through first – he used the new telegraph in Cairo. His scoops so delighted James Gordon Bennett, the manager and, later, owner of the paper, that Stanley was given a permanent job as a staff reporter. He had risen from workhouse brat to international journalist.

Stanley was particularly intelligent and exceptionally strong – as the workhouse master had discovered to his cost. He had superhuman powers of endurance, an outstanding memory, an aptitude for languages and could sketch well. In addition, he was a good horseman, strong swimmer and an accurate shot. He relished excitement and living dangerously. He experienced three naval bombardments, 15 military battles (and had reported far more), and survived two shipwrecks. All qualities for a good explorer.

And all that before he was 28.

LOST WITHOUT TRACE
Nothing definite had been heard of Livingstone for over three years but there had been numerous rumours. One was that he had been killed by

Ngong tribesmen. Another that he was travelling up the Nile; yet another that he was nearing the Atlantic coast. There were even stories he had married a wealthy African princess and had no wish to be found. All these reports were without foundation but Bennett, the *New York Herald*'s manager, smelt a good story. From Paris, he sent for Stanley who was in Madrid covering one of the earlier Spanish Civil Wars. Stanley boarded the Paris train the same day.

Bennett promised unlimited funds but added a stipulation. Before starting the search, Stanley had to go to Egypt for the opening of the Suez Canal; then travel up the Nile to interview Sir Samuel Baker who was preparing for an expedition to the Sudan. Stanley had then to go to Jerusalem to report on recent excavations and after that travel to Constantinople (now Istanbul). He then had to proceed to the Crimea battlefields and afterwards go, via Georgia, the Caspian Sea and Teheran, to the Persian Gulf. Having arrived there, he was to take a ship to Karachi and then cross to Zanzibar to prepare for the expedition. Bennett was a man who expected value for his money.

If Bennett was as anxious to find Livingstone as he claimed, these time-delaying requirements seem strange, but, for Stanley, they proved fortunate. Because of the time they took, it was a year before he could begin his trek through the African bush. Had he started any earlier, it is likely he would have missed Livingstone and the expedition would have been a complete – and very expensive – failure.

❋ ❋ ❋*SUMMARY* ❋ ❋ ❋

- Livingstone set out on what was to be his last expedition early in 1867. He sighted Lake Tanganyika, previously discovered by Burton and Speke, and discovered Lakes Moero and Bengweulu.

- He travelled to Ujiji despite ill health but found promised food, medical supplies and mail had not arrived.

- After recuperation, Livingstone set out to find the Lualaba but hopes of discovering it was the source of the Nile were dashed. Declining health forced him to return to Ujiji.

- Stanley had been brought up in a workhouse from which he absconded. He lived a varied and adventurous life before becoming a reporter for a popular American newspaper.

10 Stanley in Africa, 1871-72

ARRIVAL IN ZANZIBAR

Stanley's boat from Karachi sailed into Zanzibar harbour on 6 January 1871 and anchored among the picturesque dhows, their beauty belying the evil trade in which most were engaged.

Stanley knew nothing of Africa save what he had learnt as a war reporter in Abyssinia. No maps of the Interior existed; all he had were the reports of the previous explorers, Burton and Speke, which gave limited guidance on necessary supplies and the main snags likely to arise. From these scanty records, Stanley knew that he was entering a hazardous and difficult country with a vicious climate – just the sort of territory which appealed to his love of danger and sense of adventure.

Following the pattern established by expeditions before him, Stanley equipped his caravan on Zanzibar island, the only place where supplies were available. It was no mean task and took a good six weeks. It involved purchasing sufficient quantities for a two-year journey of rice, flour, tinned meat, candles, soap, pots, pans, coffee and tea together with axes, **pangas**, hatchets and butcher's knives. These had to be packed in containers which could withstand rough transportation. A range of weapons ranging from small single-barrelled pistols to cumbersome elephant rifles, plus an adequate supply of ammunition, also had to be included. These were needed not only for protection but also for killing wild game. Good shooting by day meant an adequate meal at night – a bad shot usually meant that it was the animal who had the meal.

KEYWORD

Pangas are weighty broad-bladed sharp implements about two feet (65 cm) long with a wooden handle and are common throughout East Africa. Similar to machetes, they are used both as tools and as weapons.

The firearms were supplemented by a collection of swords, battle-axes, spears and daggers. Tents and collapsible boats were also included. Unlike Livingstone, Stanley did not believe in travelling light and relying on local benevolence.

In order to barter for fresh water, eggs and vegetables along the route – and to use as **tributes** – Stanley took several thousand yards of material ranging from calico to fine muslin, more than a million coloured beads and necklaces made of coral, glass and china, and several hundred pounds of brass wire. He also included a wide range of 'personal' items such as his own bath, campbed, Persian carpet, table, crockery and cutlery – even a silver teapot and silver goblets. He also had to take those essential items for any explorer – sextant, compass, sounding line, lanterns and a medicine chest with, among other items, a good supply of quinine. A medical handbook and a Bible were also included together with a dog whip to keep his bearers in order – unlike Livingstone, Stanley believed that recalcitrance should be met with retribution, not compassion.

KEYWORDS

Tributes were 'payments' demanded by local tribes for permission to pass through their territory.

Bagamoyo (6.28S, 38.55E), 45 miles north of Dar es Salaam, is a historic seaport; formerly a slave-trading depot and terminus of Arab caravans from Ujiji. It was the first capital of the German East Africa Co. 1887–91.

The loads weighed over 6 tonnes and nearly 30 donkeys were needed to carry them. Two horses and a guard dog were also acquired. Stanley then recruited a retinue of nearly 200 men, including porters, guards, gun-bearers, a carpenter, cook and a tailor. He also enlisted three African 'sergeants' and two European 'lieutenants'.

The complete caravan had to be shipped across the short stretch of water to **Bagamoyo** on the Tanzanian coast. Stanley planned to make his way upcountry to Ujiji, on the banks of Lake Tanganyika, where he hoped to pick up information concerning Livingstone's whereabouts.

Stanley's complete entourage was divided into five separate parties which left on different dates in February and March. Farquhar, one of his European lieutenants, took charge of one; Shaw, his other lieutenant, commanded another. Two others were led by tribal headmen. Each party planned to follow the well-established Arab trading route to Simbamwenni, from there to Mwapwa and then up to **Tabora** before making the final trek across to Ujiji. The Portuguese and Arabs had 'worked' the route for more than a century, trading cloth and beads for slaves. The parties faced a journey first through the forested coastal region, a climb of 4,000 feet (1200 m)

KEYWORD

Tabora (5.2S, 32.57E) originally called Unyan-yembe, this was the most important trade link between the coast and the Congo before European intervention. It has retained some of its importance as the junction between the east–west Dar es Salaam to Ujiji railway, and the spur line northwards to Lake Victoria.

over the Usagara mountains and, finally, a trek across the semi-desert of the central plain thick with its thorn bush and cacti which gave little protection from the unforgiving sun. Much the same route is followed today by the railway as it makes its way from Dar es Salaam up to Kigoma on the shores of Lake Tanganyika. But there was no railway in 1871. Stanley's parties had to go the whole way on foot, carrying their supplies with them.

THE SEARCH BEGINS

Stanley left Bagamoyo in March 1871. It took nearly a month to reach Simbamwenni – named after the lions (in Swahili, *Simba*) which plagued the area. He was cheered by news from an Arab caravan that Livingstone had been seen at Ujiji making preparations to trek westwards. Stanley had planned to rest at Simbamwenni for two days, but the start of the monsoons, which turned dried-up gullies into impassable swamps miles wide and rivers into raging torrents, forced him to remain longer.

As soon as the rain eased, Stanley set out for Mwapwa, 70 miles (113 km) away. Early in May he met Farquhar's party which was in a sad state. Farquhar himself was suffering from elephantiasis, a common condition in Africa. Minute worms block the lymphatic vessels causing extreme enlargement of the limbs and preventing movement. He had to be carried everywhere and had traded most of his stores to buy luxury foods for himself. All except one of his donkeys had died from overwork. The few followers who had not deserted him were sullen and morose from his constant cursing and beatings.

He found Shaw in little better condition, suffering from constant bouts of malaria. Chronically depressed, he found fault with everything. An argument over breakfast one morning caused Stanley to knock him down and dump him outside the camp with instructions to find his own way back home. A contrite Shaw was later readmitted to the party.

Weather made progress nearly impossible. Everything was permanently sodden from rain. Metal had to be protected against rust. Ants, centipedes, weevils and all manner of other insects got into food supplies. Stagnant pools and marshes left by the rains became hyperactive breeding grounds for mosquitoes – and consequently for malaria. A constant watch had to be kept for scorpions; these creep inside boots and under blankets and, with one excruciating sting, could cripple a man for days.

Mwapwa was reached 57 days after leaving the coast. By this time, Farquhar was too sick to go any further and a number of bearers were dead or had deserted – as had the cook after being flogged for stealing. Ten of the 27 donkeys had also died. Both horses had succumbed to tsetse flies; the dog had also died. Many of the remaining men were sick from fever and dysentery.

Stanley left Mwapwa after five days' rest leaving behind a stock of supplies to be picked up on his return. He now had to battle across scorching, almost waterless semi-desert country where temperatures approached 120 degrees. Smallpox began to take its toll among the bearers and Stanley himself began to suffer successive attacks of fever and dysentery. The going got so tough that his bearers threatened to revolt. Stanley solved the problem by threatening to flog anyone who refused to continue.

Stanley arrived at Tabora in June having taken just over three months to cover 525 miles (845 km). He set up his rest camp – fortunately, as it was to turn out, some distance outside the town. Reports from caravans coming from Ujiji confirmed that Livingstone had recovered from illness and was heading west; also that he had lost most of the supplies he used for bartering. Farquhar, who had remained at Mwapwa, was reported dead whilst Shaw, who was suffering from advanced syphilis, was losing his sanity. Stanley showed him considerable compassion and nursed him day after day despite his own repeated attacks of fever.

In Tabora, Stanley met with a major problem – one which his critics were to exploit in later years. The road to Ujiji was blocked by a notorious bandit named Mirambo. An attack on a village where Mirambo was thought to be hiding proved abortive – Mirambo had left several days earlier. News that he had attacked an incoming caravan, killing all the Arabs and capturing their supplies and 300 slaves did nothing to improve morale. In August, Mirambo attacked and burned Tabora itself, but Stanley's choice of camp outside town saved him and his party.

Stanley solved the Mirambo problem by forming a 'flying' caravan. Carrying limited supplies, he headed south-west, outflanked Mirambo, then cut back north-west to the main route. He left Shaw in Tabora – he was, shortly afterwards, to achieve the questionable distinction of being the first white man to die and be buried there. The manoeuvre proved successful, and Stanley was excited to hear that a man answering Livingstone's description had recently been seen in Ujiji, though he was reported to be very sick indeed. Stanley regrouped his men and forced-marched them towards Ujiji.

THE MEETING WITH LIVINGSTONE
At midday on Friday 3 November (some reports give different dates), Stanley sighted Ujiji. The party had taken 236 days to cover 975 miles

(1,570 km). Stanley's men descended on the town firing rifles and banging drums, most of the village turning out to witness the arrival. Susi, Livingstone's personal servant, detached himself from the crowd and formally welcomed Stanley, leading him through the lines of onlookers to Livingstone. It was then that Stanley made his historic greeting.

Livingstone had only been back in Ujiji a fortnight. All except a handful of his bearers had deserted him, he was seriously ill and virtually destitute. Stanley was able to provide him with desperately needed supplies and medicines. Over the next few weeks whilst Livingstone's health slowly improved, the two became very close friends.

Stanley urged Livingstone to return to England with him, but he refused. The two compromised by agreeing to explore the western shores of Lake Tanganyika before travelling together back to Tabora. Along the coast of the lake, the two men met several groups of hostile natives: Stanley was all for solving the problem with a few well-aimed bullets but the proposal did not appeal to his missionary colleague and Stanley deferred to his wishes. On reaching Tabora, Stanley gave Livingstone a large part of his stores. It was there that the two men finally parted to go their separate ways – Stanley back to the coast to file his press reports and Livingstone back to continue exploration westwards. Both men were deeply upset at the parting. Stanley later admitted to crying 'like a child of eight'.

STANLEY'S JOURNEY HOME

On the return journey to the coast Stanley had again to battle against the monsoons, struggling through horrendous downpours of rain, fording rivers in flood, crossing 30-mile (48 km) wide swamps – and coping with huge swarms of mosquitoes. Malaria was rife. Nevertheless, he managed to make very good time considering the conditions and in April 1872 reached Mwapwa, where Farquhar had died. Although there was no trace of the body, Stanley built a stone memorial to him. It was whilst he was resting there that Stanley first heard that a 'Livingstone Relief Party' had come out from England. It had arrived in Bagamoyo a week before

Stanley who reached there on 6 May, 53 days
after leaving Tabora. Stanley had been on **safari**
for a total of 411 days and, during that time, had
trudged well over 2,000 miles (3,200 km).

KEYWORD

Safari is the Swahili
word meaning 'journey'
– any sort of journey. It
is not limited to journeys
concentrating on 'game-
spotting'.

At all the ports on his way back to England,
Stanley was hailed as a hero but he was bitterly
disappointed at his reception in England. Not
only had his greeting on meeting Livingstone already become a standing
joke, but various interests conspired to deride and defame him. The new
President of the Royal Geographical Society, Major General Sir Henry
Creswicke Rawlinson, was extremely annoyed: his own relief mission had
been upstaged by Stanley's; Livingstone's rescue had been financed by a
foreign newspaper; and it had been led by a man whom he regarded as
the very epitome of an arrogant, brash American whose writings were
nothing more than sensational journalism containing nothing of
scientific or geographic interest. Ironically, despite Stanley's own claims
otherwise, he was still legally a Briton. He did not become a naturalized
American until 1885.

Bennett, of the *New York Herald*, also played down Stanley's
achievement. He considered that because it was he, Bennett, who had
instigated and financed Stanley's expedition, it was he who should
receive the accolades which ultimately were accorded to Stanley. The *New
York Sun* and the *New York Tribune* both ran deprecating articles
accusing Stanley of being a cheat and a fraud. The *Tribune* even sank to
belittling Stanley's ungainly physical appearance. Nevertheless, Stanley
was invited to give many public addresses after his return. Unfortunately,
he had an uncanny aptitude of saying the wrong thing, to the wrong
group, in the wrong way, at the wrong time. That did not endear him to
the public.

Despite the jealousy and the conspiracies against him, Stanley was
accorded great honours. The Royal Geographical Society, despite the
earlier ridicule by its President, awarded him the society's Victorian

Medal. He was praised by Queen Victoria herself who presented him with a magnificent gold snuff box inlaid with blue enamel and encrusted with the royal 'VR' cipher in diamonds, emeralds and rubies. He received invitations to all the best houses and was banqueted by innumerable societies. One of the most treasured gifts he received was a silver locket from Livingstone's eldest daughter.

Despite all the honours and awards, Stanley never forgot the vilification which he received from so many quarters. It seemed the embodiment of the rejection by society which had plagued him since his days in the workhouse.

Perhaps the biggest paradox of Stanley's life is that his greatest achievements came *after* Livingstone died. When the razzmatazz of his return had died down, Stanley decided to devote his life to finishing Livingstone's work. He returned to Central Africa and discovered that the Lualaba – the river which Livingstone had thought to be the source of the Nile – was in fact a tributary of the massive River Congo. He was successful in getting missionaries into Uganda. Rebuffed by little interest from America and Britain, he accepted Belgian support to explore the Congo itself where he was instrumental in setting up the Congo Free State, becoming its first Governor.

A final incongruity was that this man who became a naturalized American in 1885, renaturalized as British in 1892 – only seven years later – and became again a citizen of the country which had so often and so cruelly rebuffed him in his earlier years

He was knighted in 1899 and for five years – from 1895 to 1900 – was the Member of Parliament for North Lambeth.

He died 10 May 1904.

* * *SUMMARY* * *

- Stanley reached Zanzibar in January 1871 where he made extensive preparations for his search for Livingstone.

- After sailing to Bagamoyo, Stanley's party split into five groups, each initially travelling separately.

- Farquhar, leader of one group, became very ill with elephantiasis and had to be left behind at Mwapwa where he later died. Shaw, leader of another group, died at Tabora.

- The Tabora–Ujiji route was blocked by the notorious bandit Mirambo. Stanley outflanked him and reached Ujiji where he met Livingstone whose condition was desperate.

- Livingstone and Stanley, although very different men, became great friends but Livingstone refused to return to England with him.

- Back in England, Stanley received many honours but also much ridicule.

- He later returned to explore the Congo, and eventually served as a Member of Parliament at Westminster.

Livingstone's final days, 1872–74

THE LAST JOURNEY

After Stanley's departure, Livingstone was determined to make one further expedition into the territory west of Lake Tanganyika. He planned to travel round the southern tips of Lakes Tanganyika and Bangweolo, then out to the copper mines of Katanga and beyond. He wrote that the longed-for end of his journeys was in sight. Unfortunately, he never achieved that end.

Stanley's return journey to the coast took longer than anticipated and this delayed the arrival of the new men he had promised to send up from Zanzibar. Livingstone spent the time writing letters and updating his journal. His entry for the 31 May 1872 shows that he already suspected that the Lualaba River was the not source of the Nile and that it was linked to the Congo after all – though this was something he never managed to confirm. He continued to be sickened by the activities of the slave-traders and the killing that went with it. Describing a chance visit to a deserted village, he wrote:

> Wherever we took a walk, human skeletons were seen in every direction, and it was painfully interesting to observe the different postures in which the poor wretches had breathed their last. A whole heap had been thrown down a slope behind a village where the fugitives often crossed the river from the east. Many had ended their misery under shady trees, others under projecting crags in the hills, while others lay in their huts with closed doors, which when opened disclosed the mouldering corpses with the poor rags round their loins, the skull fallen off the pillow, the little skeleton of the child, that had perished first, rolled up in a mat between two large skeletons. The sight of this desert, but eighteen months ago a well-peopled valley, now literally strewn with human bones, forced the conviction upon us that the destruction of human life constitutes but a

small portion of the waste, and made us feel that unless the slave-trade – that monster iniquity which has so long brooded over Africa – is put down, lawful commerce cannot be established.

He heard that Sir Roderick Murchison, always one of his closest friends and staunchest supporters, had died. He felt the loss deeply. He would have been even more saddened had he known that, at the Royal Geographical Society, Murchison had been succeeded by Rawlinson, the man who was so ungenerous in his attitude towards Stanley.

Livingstone commenced his final journey in August 1872. By October, he had reached Lake Tanganyika. Illness was again taking its toll, both of the bearers and of Livingstone, but he struggled on to Lake Bangweolo, reaching it in January 1873. The rainy season was now at its height, the quagmires, the flooded streams and muddy landslips making progress very difficult. The humidity was stifling and the unceasing rain made it impossible to dry anything out. Choleraic-type fevers now became an additional problem.

Livingstone's physical condition, already low, began to show sharp deterioration. By early April, he was pitifully weak from the continuous bleeding from his bowels. By the end of the month, he was near exhaustion and had to be carried everywhere. On 27 April 1873, he recorded in his journal that he had reached the banks of the River Molilamo. Those were the last words he ever wrote.

After resting for two days, the party moved on with Livingstone – only semi-conscious and in excruciating pain – being carried by bearers. Eventually, the party approached the old village of Chief Chitambo on the southern shores of Lake Bangweolo in present-day Zambia. A crude hut was built and Livingstone was laid on a rough bed. The next day he rested peaceably enough except for a few rambling questions.

During the early hours of the following day, he died.

In April 1874, 11 months after his death, Livingstone's corpse arrived in England escorted by the faithful Chuma and Susi. Injuries to the left arm caused by the lion attack so many years previously enabled the body to be formally identified. The corpse was given a hero's welcome but Chuma – who was to be a pall-bearer at Livingstone's funeral – and his friends received little praise and no reward from a parsimonious British government. On a national day of mourning in 1874, Livingstone was buried in Westminster Abbey.

He is the only explorer ever to be accorded that distinction.

* * *SUMMARY* * *

- After Stanley's departure, Livingstone resumed exploration to the west.

- As he neared Chitambo's village, his condition became critical.

- He died 1 May 1873 and is buried in Westminster Abbey.

12 Livingstone's legacy

Livingstone died a disappointed man, his hopes and ambitions unfulfilled. Despite his devotion to the task – he only had two home leaves in 30 years – he had failed to discover the source of the Nile and had not succeeded in opening a highway into the Interior for European immigration. Commercial links with Europe had not materialized and critics accused him of having failed as a missionary, as a husband and as a father. He considered that his work had served only to aid the slavers, not to destroy them. He had once said he would 'open up a path into the Interior – or perish'. As death approached, it seemed that he had *not* opened the path, but *had* perished in the attempt. But for the dramatic circumstances of his death and the ongoing joke of Stanley's greeting, it is possible that most of us today would have no greater knowledge of Livingstone's life than we have of those of the other great explorers of that era.

Is this a fair assessment of the man's achievements – and, if not, how can we more fairly evaluate his work and life?

HIS CONTRIBUTION TO GEOGRAPHIC AND SCIENTIFIC KNOWLEDGE

Although there was a succession of explorers in Africa in the nineteenth century, Livingstone was the first and set the pattern that others followed. During his 30 years in Africa he tramped

KEY FACT

Other great explorers in central Africa include Lieutenant Verney Cameron who met the party carrying Livingstone's body at Tabora – he was the first European to cross Equatorial Africa and originated the idea of a Cape to Cairo railway; Sir Richard Burton, fluent in 25 languages and over 40 dialects and who with John Speke discovered Lake Tanganyika in 1858. Speke, in the same year, also discovered Lake Victoria, solving the problem of the source of the Nile; Sir Samuel Baker who discovered Lake Albert in 1864; Italian-born Frenchman Pierre Brazza, after whom Brazzaville is named, who carried out major explorations in the Congo; Alexandre Serpa Pinta of Portugal, performed outstanding work in mapping much of the previously unexplored Interior.

across more than a third of the vast continent, venturing into areas no European had been before. He discovered Lakes 'Ngami, Shirwa, Nyasa, Moero and Bangweolo. He was the first European to reach the Victoria Falls, and the first to travel the entire length – all 470 miles (756 km) – of Lake Tanganyika.

Portuguese mariners had sailed the African coasts for more than four centuries. They had mapped the ports and trading posts but the fever-ridden Interior remained a mystery. It was Livingstone's researches, sketches and published books which filled in the vast cartographical void of central and eastern Africa. His work in mapping the upper reaches of the Zambezi and its associated tributaries proved particularly valuable. Each important location was determined with the utmost precision and his detailed records of geological and hydrographical data, together with his notes on flora and fauna, made an immense impression on contemporary scientists. Charts based on his observations remained virtually unchanged until well into the twentieth century.

In the medical field, Livingstone's use of quinine as a means of controlling malaria had far-reaching significance and was the only effective remedy for many years. It alone enabled the explorers who followed in his footsteps – and hundreds of later settlers – to survive the dreaded and often fatal fever. He showed that Africa was not necessarily the white man's grave.

LIVINGSTONE'S INFLUENCE ON COMMERCE

Although Livingstone did not live to see it, his comments on Africa's potential as a source of primary products revealed to the world the enormous commercial potential of areas previously considered barren desert. The realization that Africa could become a valuable alternative to India as a source of supplies, as well as forming a huge market in its own right, led Britain, France, Belgium, Germany and Italy to become active in promoting commercial schemes. Unfortunately, it was not foreseen that trading in many of the commodities in which Africa had natural advantages – for example, copper, cotton, tea, coffee, cocoa, tobacco and maize – would ultimately mean competing in world markets, facing stiff foreign competition and battling with internationally determined price levels. Thus, when world overproduction in more recent years meant drastic price reductions and radical cutbacks in production, several African countries were so badly hit that they have never effectively recovered. Also, the agricultural potential together with the discovery of mineral resources – such as diamonds, copper, iron and oil – resulted in their exploitation by expatriate interests in a manner hardly advantageous to African people. This development Livingstone did not foresee when he wrote of European entry to Africa 'there is no end to totally uncultivated land … far from being an intrusion, it would be a benefit (to Africans) to have a community ready to trade'. He made the world aware of the profusion of population, of the rich resources of the Interior and of their potential for commercial development – but he saw Europe not as the *exploiter* of the African resources, but as the *exporter* of job opportunities.

Was it naïve of Livingstone to think that there could be commercial development without commercial exploitation? Was he being unrealistic in hoping for large-scale commercial development overnight or for racial integration without racial prejudice and domination? Or was he just ahead of his time?

POLITICAL AND SOCIAL CONSEQUENCES

The revelations of Livingstone and of the other explorers were largely responsible for Leopold II of Belgium convening the 1876 Brussels Conference where leading explorers, geographers and politicians discussed the future of sub-Saharan Africa. This apparently innocuously inspired debate sparked off resentment and jealousy among other nations at what emerged as an expression of Belgian imperialist ambitions. It led to the unholy 'scramble for Africa' and a redrawing of the political map. Between 1880 and the end of the nineteenth century the 'African cake', as Leopold described it, was carved up between five European powers. It gave them 30 new colonies and protectorates,

10 million square miles (2,600 million hectares) of new territory and millions of new subjects. The data Livingstone gathered on his Zambezi expedition became important factors in the creation in 1893 of the British Central African Protectorate, which became Nyasaland in 1897 and Malawi in 1966. To Livingstone's three Cs – Commerce, Christianity and Civilization – a fourth C was added, namely Conquest. Unfortunately, the boundaries superimposed on the new countries were a reflection of political interests, not of criteria which might have better served the interests of Africa and its people.

THE SLAVE TRADE

Livingstone's condemnation of the slave trade in southern Africa publicized its existence to the world. The West Coast trade had been effectively curbed by Wilberforce and others, but the extent of the problem in other parts of Africa had been little appreciated. Livingstone awakened the world to its continued existence. Negligible until the mid-eighteenth century, the development of plantations in Zanzibar and its surrounding islands, of sugar and coffee plantations in Mauritius and Réunion and the increased demand from sugar plantations in Brazil, led to a phenomenal growth in the East African slave trade with more than 70,000 being exported annually. Livingstone's disclosures prompted mention of the evils in a Queen's Speech, led to a Royal Commission and a Parliamentary Select Committee. The result was a treaty, negotiated with the Sultan of Zanzibar, prohibiting the sea transportation of slaves along a 1,000-mile (1,609 km) coastline. Unfortunately, the sea routes were replaced with routes overland, subjecting the captives to even greater horrors. It was many years before slavery was – at least officially – universally abolished. The last country to do so was the Arabian Peninsular and that as recently as 1970. But slavery, sadly, still exists. Recent estimates by Christian Solidarity International suggest that in just one pocket alone – the central Sudan – between 14,000 and 42,000 Dinka tribes-women (exact figures are impossible to obtain) have been enslaved over the past ten years alone. Their menfolk have been killed, their villages burnt, their crops destroyed. Nothing changes.

HIS MISSIONARY ACHIEVEMENTS

No assessment of David Livingstone would be complete without reference to his missionary work. He laid no claim to being an academic divine: his theology, both written and expressed, was limited to a reiteration rather than a reinterpretation of conventional Christian doctrine. He believed, essentially, in a basic and pragmatic approach to religion. He had as little time for pious platitudes, purposeless idolization and needless ritual as for those who 'utter magnificent words ... without leaving one permanent trace of their labours in the belief and worship of the people'. His views may seem a harsh criticism of the significant social and religious contribution the High Church did in fact make in Africa, but it must be remembered that Livingstone was *not* a High Church man.

Although not a success as a conventional missionary, Livingstone had great success in inspiring young men to take up missionary work and, although he himself saw only the failure of the Shiré River mission, his efforts were a major factor in the subsequent establishment of missions throughout Africa. It was he who first saw the great need to expand the work into the Interior. He remained critical to his dying day of the 'colonial style' missionaries in the Cape whom he described as 'missionaries to the heathen who never march into heathen territory'. He was essentially his own man, prepared to say what he thought and to stick out for doing things the way he saw appropriate. Though strongly criticized for concentrating on exploration rather than missionary work, he remained adamant in his view that, once the Interior had been opened up by exploration and tempered by European civilization, properly organized missions could be established and that conversions in their thousands would follow.

Preaching in and through the **vernacular** language has always been an outstanding characteristic of Christian missionary work. Dr Moffat, in his translation of the Scriptures, was at the heart of that tradition, as was Livingstone's own practice of preaching in the local language and recruiting local agents. But what was its long-term influence?

> **KEYWORD**
>
> A vernacular language is the commonly spoken language or dialect of a particular people or place.

One strong argument is that the emphasis on the vernacular enabled the African Church to divorce itself from Western modes of thought, and ultimately led to Africans assuming prominent leadership roles both in Church and in government. This suggests that the missions were crucial to the evolution of African nationalism and helped to undermine imperialistic domination. However, if two developments occur contemporaneously, caution must be exercised in assigning one as the cause of the other. It is debatable whether African nationalism would have emerged so strongly had vernacular languages not been given such an important role in African churches.

What did Livingstone really mean by 'civilization' – a term which probably meant something different to everyone who used it? Livingstone may have given a clue in a confidential letter to Professor Sedgwick of Cambridge, when he wrote 'but what I can tell to none is this. I hope (my explorations) may result in an English colony in the healthy highlands of Central Africa'. The establishment of *a colony* is one thing: that of *colonial rule* is another. Livingstone never lost faith in the competence of Africans, ultimately, to handle their own affairs, believing wholeheartedly in their ability to enter the modern world as the equals of white men. 'I have no fears' he wrote, 'as to the mental and moral capacity of the Africans for civilisation and upward progress, capable of holding an honourable rank in the family of man'. So, was he associating 'civilization' with colonization and extension of empire, or was he thinking more in terms of the rule of law and a decent life for everyone? Whichever, he certainly saw a vernacular-based Church as the primary instrument in achieving his vision.

LIVINGSTONE THE MAN

It is difficult in these days of easy travel, modern medicines and organized itineraries to appreciate the sheer courage needed in Livingstone's day to undertake – without any backup – the tasks he set himself. To go into dark, impenetrable forest or across desolate bush where no white man had been before, not knowing what dangers might await in terms of hostile tribes, dangerous animals, endemic disease and lack of water and food, must have demanded a bravery few of us can claim to possess. It also demanded a remarkable physical constitution. To hike a few miles is one thing; to fight one's way across *a continent*, is altogether another.

Nor is it easy to appreciate the sheer time-spans involved and the incredible determination that must have been required to see the tasks through. To drive from the Cape to Kuruman along modern tarmac roads in a few hours, or to cruise the Zambezi in air-conditioned luxury, is a very different proposition from that which faced the early explorers, bumping along with their ox-drawn wagons in scorching heat, literally carving their way through bush, making no more than a few miles an hour at best.

Livingstone was, essentially, an individualist. He was incapable of leading his peers and was unwilling to be led by them. Right from his early years, Livingstone exhibited one quality beyond all others. It was that he knew what he wanted, where he was going and what he wanted to achieve. He was not prepared to consider any contrary idea.

Perhaps, in order to achieve great things in this life, such qualities are necessary. But a price has to be paid. In Livingstone's case, his single-mindedness turned colleagues into critics, caused problems which could have been avoided and made him a difficult – some would say impossible – man to work with.

Was he a dogmatic egoist who brooked no complaint? Perhaps the view of one who knew him far better than most gives us a clue – namely Henry Morton Stanley, a man of altogether different attitude and outlook and who could be pardoned for being critical. He wrote that, in Livingstone, he expected to find 'a crusty misanthrope'. Instead, he found a man who was as tender-hearted as he was brave, a skilled explorer to be admired and an outstanding preacher who was able to generate the most devoted loyalty among his followers. He was a man full of sympathy and humanity, a person who was pacific in his approach but was no pacifist, one who was admired even by slave-traders who described him as 'that very great doctor'.

Livingstone's life presents its enigmas. What he achieved was not what he set out to achieve. Although he regarded himself first and foremost as a missionary, exploration not proselytization became his priority. To be fair, in 'opening up' Africa, he hoped others would succeed as missionaries in a way which, for him, had not been possible. It was not so much the end which changed, but the means to that end.

Perhaps the greatest paradox of his life is that he was, at the same time, the precursor both of African nationalism and of European imperialism.

* * *SUMMARY* * *

- Livingstone died a disappointed man, little realizing how the seeds he had sown would blossom.

- He made immense contributions to geographic and scientific knowledge, the development of commerce, the (ultimate) eradication of the slave trade in Africa and the development of missions, mission schools and mission hospitals.

- His work also had significant political repercussions.

- Above all else, he was an individualist who would let no one stand in his way in the pursuit of his goals.

SELECT BIBLIOGRAPHY

STANDARD BIOGRAPHIES OF LIVINGSTONE

Blaikie, W. G. *The Personal Life of David Livingstone*, John Murray (1880). This book still makes excellent reading. Written only a few years after Livingstone's death, it lacks objectivity but captures the euphoria of the time.

Nicholls, D. *David Livingstone*, Sutton Publishing (1998).

Ross, D. *The Story of David Livingstone*, Corbie – Waverley Books (2001). A readable, short account for children of Livingstone's life.

Seaver, G. *David Livingstone – His Life and Letters*, Butterworth (1957). A detailed, authoritative, objective and easily readable account of Livingstone's life and work.

Wellman, S. *David Livingstone: Missionary and Explorer*, Barbour Publishing (1995).

ACCOUNTS OF PARTICULAR ASPECTS OF LIVINGSTONE'S LIFE

Coupland, R. *Livingstone's Last Journey*, Collins (1945).

Livingstone, D. *Missionary Travels and Researches in South Africa* (1857).

Livingstone, D. *Narrative of an Expedition to the Zambezi and its Tributaries and of the Discovery of Lakes Shirwa and Nyassa* (1865).

Livingstone, D. et al. *Expedition to the Zambezi*, Gerald Duckworth (2001).

Monk, W. (ed.) *Dr Livingstone's Cambridge Lectures* (1858).

Waller, H. (ed.) *The Last Journals of David Livingstone in Central Africa from 1865 to his Death*, 2 vol. (1874).

ACCOUNTS OF THE BROADER BACKGROUND WITHIN WHICH LIVINGSTONE WORKED

Browne, S. (ed.) *Heralds of Health – The Saga of Christian Medical Initiatives*, Christian Medical Fellowship (1985)

Hastings, I. *The Church in Africa 1450–1950*, Clarendon Press (1994)

Pakenham, T. *The Scramble for Africa*, Weidenfeld and Nicolson (1991)

Shilliington, K. *History of Africa*, Macmillan Educational (revd edn 1995)

ACCOUNTS OF STANLEY'S LIFE

Anstruther, I. *I Presume – H. M. Stanley, Triumph and Disaster*, Allen Sutton Publishing (1956)

Hind, F. *H. M. Stanley – The Authorized Life*, Stanley Paul and Co. (1935)

Stanley, H. M. *Through the Dark Continent*, Dover Publications (1994) (new edition of the 1899 edition)

WEBSITE ADDRESSES

For useful information concerning the Livingstone Institute and Museum at Blantyre, Glasgow, together with a list of other relevant web addresses, visit **www.biggar-net.co.uk/livingstone**

INDEX